TRILOGY
CHRISTIAN
PUBLISHING

by formally affirming them, but by imposing concrete restraints on government. These limitations ensure both our political and economic liberty. In their book *The Three Cs That Made America Great: Christianity, Capitalism, and the Constitution*, Mike Huckabee and Steve Feazel masterfully demonstrate the interrelationship between these ideas and institutions and how America's uniqueness is dependent on all three. This book will be more than an informative read. It can serve as a teaching guide to better comprehend specific moments in our nation's history that exemplified these ideals.

—David Limbaugh

I've lived both the American Nightmare and the American Dream. I was poor, lacked an education, caught up in petty crime, drugs, was a welfare cheat, and had four abortions as a method of birth control. After finding Christ, forgiveness, and the power to live a life free from the past, I found that America worked for me too. The organization I founded and currently lead is UrbanCURE (Center for Urban Renewal and Education), and it's built on and promotes the very things my long-time friend Mike Huckabee and coauthor Steve Feazel write about in *The Three Cs That Made America Great: Christianity, Capitalism, and the Constitution*. I know firsthand how Christianity overcomes our past, the power of capitalism to truly liberate us financially, and the genius of the Constitution to give a framework for our freedom. You will enjoy and be enlightened by this fact-filled book!"

—Star Parker
Founder/President of UrbanCURE, author, speaker, and best-selling author

I have had the great honor to travel with Mike Huckabee to Israel and have stood shoulder to shoulder with him fighting for religious liberty across the United States. Mike Huckabee is a good friend I can always count on to clearly communicate truth and to stand for what is right no matter the consequences. Mike and Steve Feazel have given Americans skeptical of our exceptionalism a book filled with great stories of those who truly made America great. But more than great stories, this must-read book is filled with the facts and documentation that a lawyer like me appreciates in a style that anyone can read and understand.

—Mathew D. Staver, Esq., BCS
Founder and chairman of Liberty Counsel, former dean and professor of law
at Liberty University School Law School, Constitutional law expert

My ninety-three-year-old Marine daddy, Corporal Curley Gatlin, worked at dirty, hot, stinkin', low-paying jobs for forty years to feed, clothe, and house my mom, Steve, Rudy, our sister LaDonna and me. He never made more than thirty thousand dollars a year in his life.

Because he and mom raised us "in the Word" and taught us to love God and country, and because they instilled in us the credo that work is noble, and because of our God-given talent, I have more money in my pocket than my daddy ever had in the bank. I've written a song about that...but enough about me.

My pal Gov. Huck has written a new book that talks about those same values: faith, hard work, and capitalism. I've read some of the "highlights." I can't wait to read the rest of the book. I know it will be a blessing and give me renewed hope during these troubled times in America! Thanks for writing it, Gov. Huck old friend.

—Larry Gatlin
Grammy-winning singer, songwriter, entertainer with the Gatlin Brothers

Huckabee and Feazel have sounded the alarm for Americans to guard their freedom of worship, free markets, and personal liberties, which are under assault by sinister forces.

—Melissa Ohden
Abortion survivor, best-selling author, and prominent pro-life speaker

Steve Feazel and Gov. Huckabee reacquaint us with the three essential pillars of our nation's founding, and of what will happen if we fail to preserve them. The bottom line? If the pillars crumble, America crumbles.

—Rebecca Hagelin
CEO of United in Purpose, conservative author and columnist

THE THREE Cs THAT MADE
AMERICA
GREAT

CHRISTIANITY ★ CAPITALISM
and the CONSTITUTION

MIKE HUCKABEE
STEVE FEAZEL

TRILOGY
CHRISTIAN PUBLISHING

TRILOGY
CHRISTIAN
PUBLISHING

Trilogy Christian Publishers
A Wholly Owned Subsidiary of Trinity Broadcasting Network
2442 Michelle Drive
Tustin, CA 92780

For information about special discounts for bulk purchases, please contact Trilogy Christian Publishing.

Design, Diane Whisner

Manufactured in the United States of America

10   9   8   7   6   5   4   3   2   1

Library of Congress Cataloging-in-Publication Data is available.

ISBN 978-1-64773-304-9
ISBN 978-1-64773-305-6 (ebook)

THE THREE Cs THAT MADE
AMERICA GREAT

CHRISTIANITY ★ CAPITALISM

and the CONSTITUTION

CONTENTS

★

FOREWORD

★

Five days a week on nationally syndicated radio and the Fox News Channel, I do my best to sound the alarm that our great country is in trouble because we have failed to understand the nature of our freedom and fully appreciate those who fought and died to preserve it. I wrote my book *Live Free or Die* to sound the alarm on what is happening in America that is undermining our future. My friend and long-time Fox News colleague Mike Huckabee and Steve Feazel have teamed up to provide a very vivid reminder of America's foundational principles in their compelling new book, *The Three Cs That Made America Great: Christianity, Capitalism, and the Constitution.*

Woven among the reminders of who our founders were, what they really believed, and why they believed it are stark comparisons between what we were intended to be and what we have become. We have steered far off course because of the corruptive influences of those who dismiss our great Republic as "just another nation" and reject the notion of American exceptionalism.

Huckabee and Feazel carefully and thoroughly document the heroes of our heritage and the unique contributions they made to create a system of government unlike any other in history.

You will be stunned by the facts they reveal about the original intentions of our educational institutions and by how radical the notion of private property rights was at the time of America's founding. The creation of our nation and its continued unparalleled excellence for almost 250 years is miraculous and arguably the result of divine intervention. This book doesn't just SAY that, it documents it.

I'm deeply saddened that many Americans, especially younger ones, don't know our history and yet are trying to radically change our country. Without knowledge of our origins and subsequent history, they are in no position to tell us where we should be headed. But if we follow their misguided prescriptions, America, as founded, will cease to exist. That's why this important book is a must-read for all those with a sincere desire to understand what DID make America great!

—Sean Hannity

Nationally syndicated radio host,
host of top-rated, in all of cable news, *Hannity* on the Fox News Channel,
and best-selling author of *Live Free or Die* and other books.

DEDICATION

★

To my six grandchildren—Chandler, Scarlett, Caroline, Huck, George, and Thatcher—with hopes that the America I grew up in will still be "land of the free and home of the brave" as they inherit it.

And to my first boss, Haskell Jones, manager of KXAR Radio in Hope, Arkansas, who saw something in a timid fourteen-year-old and gave me a chance, and whose patriotism and sense of community service were an example that imprinted my soul.

ACKNOWLEDGMENTS

★

My heartfelt thanks to coauthor Steve Feazel, who brought the concept
of this project to me, and for the friendship it's created.

Thanks to my wife, Janet,
and our two dogs, Toby and Sonic ("the boys")
who provide companionship and comfort from a
sometimes-cruel world.

And thanks to everyone at TBN who has made it possible for me to
host the TV show of my dreams, for their devotion to doing it right,
and to their publishing arm of Trilogy Publishing and their team who
have made this the smoothest and most seamless
book project I've been involved with.

—MIKE HUCKABEE

DEDICATION

★

To the memory of my brother Jack Feazel
and to the memory of my dear friend Jim Cummins,
both of whom would have enthusiastically embraced
the message of this book.

To my oldest son, Lance Feazel,
who supports the conservative message.

ACKNOWLEDGMENTS

★

I am so grateful to my coauthor, Governor Mike Huckabee.
His insights and experience in the political arena were a valuable asset
to this project. I could not have chosen a better match
or a partner given the topics covered in this book. It is indeed an
honor to call him friend and colleague. I thank my wife, Edythe, for
her wordsmith skills and literary advice. She is my first-line editor on
my writing projects. I am grateful to the Trilogy
Publishing team for believing in the message of this book.
Stacy Baker and Bryan Norris have been great to work with,
and I thank them for making this project a reality.
Our editor, Jill Jones, has done a superb job,
for which we are grateful.

—STEVE FEAZEL

INTRODUCTION

★

From a meager beginning, the United States of America became the greatest nation the world has ever known. It gained this distinction because of its wealth, generosity, ingenuity, military power, and values that celebrated the right of freedom for all men. As the greatest military power the world has seen, it did not use that power to expand its rule over weaker nations. No nation has amassed the wealth that the United States has, and no nation has been so generous with that wealth when a disaster has struck in a distant land. No other nation has executed such behavior on the world stage. In fact, at the end of World War II, the United States didn't take over the land or economies of Japan or Germany—it rebuilt them!

This powerful, great nation was unique in its interaction with other countries. What was it that made it different? Is it still in play today? The United States displayed a high character that was unmatched in history. What was the foundation from which this character came? Simply put, this nation was founded on Judeo-Christian principles that gave it a national moral conscience. This moral conscience came from Christianity and its roots. The wealth of our nation came from capitalism, which the founders allowed to be established and to flourish. They truly felt that the Christian faith and capitalism were compatible with each other. Christianity (in whatever form it was practiced) and capitalism existed in this new nation because people had the liberty to pursue them. The two were securely linked together in the Declaration of Independence: "We hold these truths to be self-evident, that all men are created equal, that they are endowed by their Creator with certain unalienable Rights, that among these are Life, Liberty and the pursuit of Happiness."

These revolutionary words launched a for-real revolutionary war, which won our nation its independence. The founders did not shy away from tying liberty to faith. For them, liberty meant the freedom to pursue wealth, not to be guaranteed wealth or even a contrived "living wage." The nations from which the colonists came were ruled by monarchs, making tyranny the norm. Tyrants care nothing for the *pursuit of happiness* for the people they rule. They only seek control and order over their subjects as they exploit them for their own power and riches. Tyrants do not see all people having equal rights. They benefit from a system where they make sure the common man has fewer rights. The concept that all men have equal rights because they are all created by God is sacrilege to the tyrant.

Conservative talk show host and author Mark Levin reveals the attitude the founders had regarding the advantage faith played in society and a nation's welfare:

> Faith is not a threat to civil society but rather vital to its survival. It encourages the individual to personally adhere to a dogma that promotes restraint, duty, and moral behavior, which not

only benefit the individual but the multitudes and society generally.[1]

Founding Father Gouverneur Morris, who is credited with being the literary composition overseer of the Constitution, could well have served as spokesman for the founders on this topic when he wrote, "Religion is the only solid Base of morals and Morals are the only possible Support of free governments."[2] The Christian faith was seen as a necessity by the founders when establishing the nation. It is a shame that such a view is not shared by our politicians today.

The ownership of property is at the heart of capitalism. It was highly valued by the founders, and they saw it tied to the Christian faith, as the words of John Adams reveal:

> The moment the idea is admitted into society that property is not as sacred as the laws of God, and that there is not a force of law and public justice to protect it, anarchy and tyranny commence. If "Thou shalt not covet" and "Thou shalt not steal" were not commandments of Heaven, they must be made inviolable precepts in every society before it can be civilized or made free.[3]

Our mother country, England, like most other European nations, was not an advocate of the common man owning property. Land was dispersed to favored nobles of the king who secured his political power. The ordinary citizen had little or no hope of owning his own land and gaining his own wealth. This fact made migration to America popular. The idea of property ownership as a part of one's basic rights was indeed an earth-shaking concept, especially when it was tied to the Creator.

The founders saw the value of religious faith as a restraint on the behavior of the people while still assuring them basic liberties. The Constitution was the instrument to restrain government to make sure liberties were not eroded. The Constitution does not overtly reference religious faith in its text except in the First Amendment, which this book will focus on in Part 3. However, the founders did not feel that their work on this document was absent the hand of God. James Madison, who is credited with being the Father of the Constitution, wrote:

> It is impossible for the man of pious reflection not to perceive in it [the Constitution] a finger of that Almighty hand which has been so frequently and signally extended to our relief in the critical stages of the revolution.[4]

The Father of the Constitution had no doubt the Father in heaven was actively involved in the drafting of this historical document. The three founding pillars of Christianity, capitalism, and Constitution are strongly tied together and must not be taken for granted. This book will reveal how important these three factors are in the history of our nation and how they made the United States the greatest nation in the history of the world.

In March of 2019, Eric Holder, the attorney general for President Obama, said that America was never great. He went on to say that it was not great when slavery existed, when women could not vote, or when gays could not marry. Never great! Really?[5] I bet the French during World War II thought the USA was great when we freed them from German occupation. One can bet the Holocaust survivors thought we were great when our troops freed them from Hitler's death camps. One can imagine many around the world have thought America was great when a lifesaving drug was created in the USA and made available around the world. One thing is for certain, if the leftists and socialists have their way, America will cease to be great, and that would be a tragedy for the world.

The book is divided into three parts. Part 1 focuses on Christianity, with a look at colonial times and how the Christian faith played a significant role in the nation's founding and subsequent history. Part 2 looks at the rise of capitalism and how the founders embraced it. It will be contrasted with the feudal system of old Europe, and capitalism's impact throughout our history will be reviewed. Part 3 examines the Constitution, how it was debated and drafted, how it was adopted, and how it has functioned down through the years. Each part will also reveal how sinister forces are attacking these three institutions. Hopefully readers will respond in a positive way to the challenge to become active in helping our nation to continue to value these three important pillars of our founding so they may continue to influence the culture and life of our country.

1

Christian Faith Comes to a New World

★

On November 9, 1620, a small ship spotted the land that would later become known as Cape Cod, Massachusetts. The passengers on this ship had spent sixty-six days on their voyage, enduring sea sickness and dangerous storms. Historically, we know them as the Pilgrims and their ship as the *Mayflower*. They had set sail from England on September 6 of that year. They made this perilous journey for one major reason: to live where they could freely practice their Christian faith as they chose. Their original destination was the northern part of Virginia, but they sought first to reach the current Hudson River area. Rough seas forced them back to the cape and finally to what they named Plymouth Rock.[1]

As one visits Plymouth Rock and walks around on the replica of the *Mayflower* moored in its harbor, it is difficult to imagine how 102 pilgrims could have crammed themselves into the ship and endured the hardship of the voyage successfully. Their faith was the motivating factor. Why did they feel the need to take such a risk?

Many historians review America's early history and classify it as a Christian nation, but could not the countries of Europe during the Pilgrims' time have claimed the same? These countries had national churches that were of Christian lineage. Couldn't these nations be called Christian? During the time of the Pilgrims, the established church had become corrupted. It sought favor with the nation's king instead of the King of kings. The church used this royal favor to enhance its power and riches. The rights of the common man were of no more concern to the church than they were to the king. The king saw the church as a useful political tool with which to control his subjects. The established church epitomized the scripture verse "having a form of godliness but denying its power" (2 Timothy 3:5 NIV).

To a very large degree, this is the battle of the current culture in America. Are we a nation of individuals, with *personal* liberties and responsibilities, or a nation of subgroups whose identity is found in race, gender, sexual preference, socioeconomic status, ethnicity, religion, or ideology? If we are collectivists and believe that we are only valuable as such to the state or its designations, we are no longer in sync with the vision of the founders who created a nation based on individual rights that were God-given but that came with God-ordained responsibilities.

In the days before we were constituted in liberty, any group that sought to pull out of the established church was dealt with, sometimes severely. An example of such an atrocity was the massacre of nearly one hundred Protestants at the bridge over the River Bann in Ireland in 1641, some twenty-one years after the Pilgrims sailed from England.[2] A group known as the Puritans who also wished to reform the Anglican Church met with little success and followed the Pilgrims to New England starting in 1630. Their numbers would swell to twenty thousand when their migration was done.[3]

The Quakers made their way to the New World, with some twenty-three thousand coming over from the northern midlands of England from 1675 to 1725. They mainly settled in the Delaware River area of what is now Pennsylvania and New Jersey.[4] The Quakers endured horrible persecution from the Church of England. Their meetings were invaded and disrupted. Troops were frequently dispatched to their meetings to execute severe beatings. Many Quaker men were put in prison and charged with fines. It is little wonder that the Quakers chose to make their way to America.[5]

Christianity in the Colonial Charters

To gain the full impact of the religious fervor held by the early colonists in America, we only need to review the charters of the colonies. A 1609 charter for the Virginia colony contained these words: "The principle effect which we can desire or expect of this action is the conversion . . . of the people in those parts unto the true worship of God and Christian religion."[6]

The Massachusetts Charter of 1629 reveals an evangelistic purpose for the colony:

> Our said people . . . be so religiously, peaceable, and civilly governed that their good life and orderly conversation may win and incite the natives of . . . that country to the knowledge and obedience of the only true God and Savior of mankind, and the Christian faith, which . . . is the principle of this plantation (colony).[7]

The 1662 North Carolina Colonial Charter expressed a sentiment similar to that of Massachusetts's founders: "Being excited with a laudable and pious zeal for the propagation of the Christian faith."[8] Other colony charters contained expressions that clearly showed their allegiance to Christianity. The colonial documents of the original thirteen colonies give overwhelming evidence the Christian faith was embraced, was practiced, and was influential in politics and culture. As time went on, many colonies created their governments out of the language that was written in their original charters. Connecticut drafted the "Fundamental Orders of Connecticut," which was the first constitution penned in America. The words in this remarkable document are very telling: "Well knowing when a people are gathered together, the word of God requires that to [maintain] the peace and union of such a people, there should [be] an orderly and decent government established according to God."[9]

Those who established colonies in the New World were not shy about their allegiance to the Christian faith and proudly proclaimed it as a vital part of their mission and basis for governing. They could not conceive of life without their faith, and they regarded it as an underlying foundation for the colony. Not only did the original documents of the colonies clearly reveal evidence of a bond to the Christian faith, but the first universities established in the colonies did the same. Five of these universities have histories that bear no resemblance to their present-day secular and morally bankrupt status.

First Colleges

The first college founded in the colonies was Harvard in the town of Cambridge, formerly known as Newtowne, near Boston in 1636. The purpose of the school was to train ministers. The words of the founders left no doubt of this:

> After God had carried us safely to New England, and we had

built our houses, provided necessaries for our livelihood, reared convenient places for God's worship, and settled the civil government; one of the next things we longed for, and looked after was to advance learning, and perpetuate it to posterity; dreading to leave an illiterate ministry to the churches, when our present ministers shall lie in the dust.[10]

Harvard takes its name from a minister named John Harvard. A statue of him sitting in a chair with an open Bible on his lap is a permanent fixture in the college's main yard. John Harvard, though a pious man, held no record of distinguished service or great accomplishments. He simply did not live long enough. He died of tuberculous on September 14, 1638, just two months shy of his thirty-first birthday. Along with four hundred books for the college library, he bequeathed half of his substantial inherited wealth to the college. In 1639 the Great and General Court established the name Harvard College in honor of the young minister's gift.[11]

The college had distinct rules that students were required to strictly follow. These rules and precepts clearly show that Harvard was indeed a Christian institution. Below are the first three Rules and Precepts of Harvard:

1. When any scholar is able to understand Tully, or such like classical Latin author extempore, and make and speak true Latin in verse and prose, and decline perfectly the paradigms of nouns and verbs in the Greek tongue: Let him then and not before be capable of admission into the college.

2. Let every student be plainly instructed, and earnestly pressed to consider well, the main end of his life and studies is, to know God and Jesus Christ which is eternal life, John

17:3, and therefore to lay Christ in the bottom, as the only foundation of all sound knowledge and learning. And seeing the Lord only giveth wisdom, let every one seriously set himself by prayer in secret to seek it of him Prov. 2, 3.

3. Every one shall so exercise himself in reading the Scriptures twice a day, that he shall be ready to give such an account of his proficiency therein, both in theoretical observations of the language, and logic, and in practical and spiritual truths, as his tutor shall require, according to his ability; seeing the entrance of the word giveth light, it giveth understanding to the simple, Psalm. 119. 130.[12]

I wonder how the students at Harvard today would fare under these rules. The early motto of Harvard was "Truth for Christ and the Church."[13] Now the motto is just "Truth," and some would debate the appropriateness of its usage. It would be fun to take a video camera to the Harvard campus today and poll students on the origins of the school they are paying almost seventy thousand dollars a year to attend.

The second college founded in the colonies was the College of William & Mary. Its name comes from King William III and Queen Mary II of England, who signed a charter for a "perpetual College of Divinity, Philosophy, Languages, and other good Arts and Sciences" in 1693. The first building was erected in 1695 even before its location town of Williamsburg, Virginia, came into existence.[14] Thomas Jefferson is an alumnus of the college, and George Washington received his surveyor's license from the school. In 1792 the college rules stated that "the students shall attend prayers in chapel at the time appointed."[15]

Modern times have not esteemed the original Christian emphasis of the college. On October of 2006, the president had a cross removed from the altar in the chapel so it would not offend people of other faiths. It was later returned in a Plexiglas case and could be placed on the altar by request. More controversy came when William & Mary hosted a "Sex Workers' Art Show" that featured monologues and performances by porn stars and strippers.[16] I would imagine the 1792 rules were no longer being enforced.

The third college, which would join the Ivy League with Harvard one day, was Yale. Its concept was developed by ten ministers who all donated books for its library. The college found its home in New Haven, Connecticut, in 1716. Its 1701 charter clearly states the purpose of the school: "Wherein Youth may be instructed in the Arts and Science who through the blessing of Almighty God may be fitted for Publick employment both in Church and Civil State."[17]

The college became known as Yale in honor of Welshman Elihu Yale of the British East India Company, who donated the proceeds from sales along with 417 books and a portrait of King George I. At one time, the college held the motto of "Christ the Word and Interpreter of the Father, our light and perfection." Today it simply uses "Light and Truth."[18] Living a Christian lifestyle was expected of early students. The college rules in 1787 stated, "All scholars are required to live a religious and blameless life according to the rules of God's Word."[19] Today, God's Word at Yale is likely paid no attention by the vast majority of students. It would be interesting to find out how many Bibles are even in the dorm rooms.

Princeton University was first known as the College of New Jersey and was founded in 1746 in Elizabeth, New Jersey. It was founded by the New Light Presbyterians. The term "New Light" refers to those enlightened by the Great Awakening. The Great Awakening produced many converts now organized into churches that were in need of clerical leadership. The purpose was to train such leaders in New Jersey instead of sending the students off to New England. In 1756 it moved its location to Princeton, New Jersey, and adopted the name of the town as its own. The most famous historic name related to the college is John Witherspoon, who served as its president from 1768 to 1794 and is the only minister to sign the Declaration of Independence.[20]

Princeton's flag displays the school's shield and motto. The open book on the shield is inscribed with *Vet. Nov. Testamentum* (Old and New Testament). The motto "Dei Sub Numine Viget" translates as "Under the Protection of God She Flourishes."[21] It is amazing that a reference to God still remains in the school's motto. Somehow it does not seem to fit with the 2005 launching of their Lesbian, Gay, Bisexual, Transgender Center.[22] Dr. Witherspoon would not likely have approved such an action.

Another colonial college destined to make its way to the Ivy League is known today as Columbia University, established in 1754 in New York City. It was first known as King's College and was brought into existence by royal charter of King George II.[23] The first president, Samuel Johnson, selected the motto "In Thy light shall we see the Light." It was taken from Psalm 36:9.[24] The college had a unique admission qualification in its early years. Prospective students had to be able to translate the Gospels from Greek to English. All students were expected to attend Sunday worship services.[25] Most students at Columbia today have probably not even read a Gospel, let alone translated it from Greek.

Faith in the Schools and the Great Awakening

Education of children in America was strongly connected to the Christian faith. *The New England Primer* was used as a textbook and was virtually a Christian catechism. The Bible was taught and used as if it were a textbook. The Founding Fathers saw education as a key to moral living and wanted public instruction to convey Christian tenets. Dr. Benjamin Rush, a signer of the Declaration of Independence, wrote: "The only foundation for a useful education in a republic is to be laid in religion. Without this there can be no virtue, and without virtue there can be no liberty, and liberty is the object and life of all republican governments."[26] Given the words of Dr. Rush, Christianity would be a welcome influence in the public school system. Sadly, this is not the case today.

July 4, 1776, is regarded as the birthday of the United States of America. If it has a birthday, then the case can be made that Christianity is its mother. The evidence for this is best seen in a spiritual phenomenon that swept the colonies like a prairie fire, known as the Great Awakening. The Great Awakening was born in a series of revivals that took place from around the mid-1730s until 1743. The Puritan minister Jonathan Edwards was a noted voice in the revivals, but the personality who attained celebrity status as the leading evangelical preacher in the movement was the British minister George Whitefield. The spiritual impact the Great Awakening had on the colonies was phenomenal, but it was not without controversy. Clergy who oversaw the old-line denominations saw the movement as a threat to their power base and control. They taught salvation was best attained by living according to the rules or discipline set forth by the church.

The Great Awakening emphasized that salvation is gained by repentance and being born again spiritually by faith. It mirrored to some degree Luther's Reformation, when he focused on salvation by faith and not the liturgy of the Catholic Church. The established denominations, such as the Anglicans and Puritans, had control over a community's religious practices. They taught one gained salvation by adherence to the rules of the church and the conduct prescribed by the church. The Great Awakening changed all this when thousands of repentant unbelievers and rekindled faithful found new spiritual life. There was a marked division among churches. A town could have a Presbyterian church, but it would have to be defined to outsiders as either "Old Light" or "New Light." The latter meant that the congregation was composed of those who received new spiritual life during the Great Awakening, and the former meant that the congregation was made up of those who continued in the old patterns.

The Great Awakening is seen by many as a revolution minus the bullets as the common man ventured to seek spiritual life apart from the ecclesiastical authority of an established church. Some felt this gave rise to the spirit of liberty that would be a factor in the American Revolution. To this end, British statesman William Knox wrote about the American drive for independence: "Every man being thus allowed to be his own Pope, he becomes disposed to wish to become his own King."[27] The meaning being that if a man can control his spiritual life, why not his political life?

No discussion of the Great Awakening would be complete without due attention given to the British preacher George Whitefield. At the age of twenty-five years, he had a powerful effect on the thousands upon thousands that heard him preach. His first visit to America was to join his friends John and Charles Wesley, fellow Anglicans who were doing missionary work in the Georgia colony. The Wesleys would later start the Methodist movement in England. It was not a productive experience. His next trip to America was in 1739 and fell during the Great Awakening. His ministry was focused in New England and the middle colonies. Nathan Cole, a Connecticut farmer who rode twelve miles on horseback to hear Whitefield preach, described what it was like to hear him:

> When I saw Mr. Whitefield come upon the Scaffold he looked almost angelical; a young, Slim. Slender, youth before some thousands of people with a bold undaunted Countenance, and my hearing how God was with him every where as he came along it Solemnized my mind; and put me into a trembling fear before he began to preach; for he looked as if he was Cloathed with authority from the Great God; *and a sweet sollome solemnity sat upon his brow*[.] And my hearing him preach, gave me a heart wound; By God's blessing: my old Foundation was broken up, and I saw that my righteousness would not save me.[28]

Whitefield would hold his meetings in the open air when churches would not let him preach or crowds were just too large to contain. Benjamin Franklin, a Founding Father who was sympathetic to the Christian faith but was not known as an ardent believer, was quite taken with Rev. Whitefield. He marveled at the preacher's impact:

> It was wonderful to see the Change soon made in the Manners of our Inhabitants; from being thoughtless or indifferent about Religion, it seem'd as if all the World were growing Religious; so

that one could not walk thro' the Town in an Evening without Hearing Psalms sung in different Families of every Street.[29]

Whitefield attracted astoundingly large crowds that would be remarkable even by today's standards. It was common for eight thousand people to come hear him preach. In Hyde Park in Boston he once drew a crowd of fifty thousand.[30] Franklin calculated twenty-five thousand heard Whitefield when he preached outside the Philadelphia Court House. Franklin, as a young printer, found Whitefield's sermons, journals, and images were among his best-selling items.[31] It is estimated that Whitefield inspired 30 percent of the printed works published in the American colonies by 1740, which was soon after his arrival.[32] This is a phenomenal accomplishment and reveals just how effective Whitefield's ministry was during the Great Awakening. On Whitefield's seventh trip to America he did not return to England. He died at the age of fifty-five on September 30, 1770, and is interred in the Presbyterian church in Newburyport, Massachusetts.

By the 1750s, George Whitefield was a household name in colonial America. The growth of the New Light portion of Christianity was strong, proven by the fact that the Puritans and Anglicans in 1760 made up 40 percent of America's congregations. By 1790, when the Constitution was being accepted, the number had decreased to 2.5 percent.[33]

The Great Awakening facilitated the emergence of the common man in the colonies that would be a factor in the coming revolution. The preachers of the Great Awakening spoke in the language of the common man. They carried no pretense or ecclesiastical rhetoric that characterized the homilies of the clergy in the established and renowned churches. Those who would light the fires of rebellion in speeches in later years would echo this approach. The Great Awakening played an important role in setting the stage for the political revolution that followed. No one believed this to be truer than John Adams, who wrote, "The Revolution was effected before the war commenced. The Revolution was in the minds and hearts of the people; a change in their religious sentiments of their duties and obligations."[34]

One thing the colonies would need in a fight against the British was unity. Unity was not an easy thing to achieve when you had thirteen colonies covering nearly one thousand miles, from New England to Georgia. The Great Awakening is credited by historians as the uniting factor that did unite the people of the colonies in a national moral consciousness. It was the bedrock foundation for the desire for liberty and the courage to pursue it.

The ministers of the colonies, both the evangelicals from the New Light and those of the Old Light, played a vital role in the promotion of the idea of independence from the British Crown. Thomas Kidd, in his book *The Great Awakening*, gives insight to this fact:

> The leaders of the evangelical movement who supported the Revolution also helped mobilize their congregations and towns and some served as chaplains in the army. Nonevangelical ministers did the same sort of work, and they often used essentially the same religious language to promote the cause. Nevertheless, evangelical ministers, especially in New England, played a critical role in generating popular support for independence.[35]

Black Robe Regiment

As the revolutionary war approached, some of the leading spokesmen for independence were the preachers. These pulpiteers were outspoken about the oppression of British rule and how the people in the colonies had fewer rights than British subjects in England. The local pastor had great influence on his community, and his opinions were often persuasive. The British were very aware of this and had a term for these prophets of liberty: the "Black Robe Regiment," in reference to the garb they wore while preaching.

It has been stated that "there is not a right asserted in the Declaration of Independence which had not been discussed by the New England clergy before 1763."[36] This is quite the accolade extended to the colonial clergy, which puts them in lockstep with the Founding Fathers. Later historians hold a similar conclusion, as seen in the words of B. F. Morris in 1864:

> The ministers of the Revolution were like their Puritan predecessors, bold and fearless in the cause of their country. No class of men contributed more to carry forward the Revolution and to achieve our independence than did the ministers. . . . [B]y their prayers, patriotic sermons, and services [they] rendered the highest assistance to the civil government, the army, and the country.[37]

Jonathan Mayhew was the pastor of West Church in Boston. He was an avid supporter of civil and religious liberty. He advanced the idea that resistance to tyranny was a Christian duty.[38] With the acclaim given to ministers, it is easy to understand why the British military despised them and actually referred to them as a regiment. Their words inflicted

40

as much, if not more, damage on the Redcoat forces than the musket balls of the Continental Army.

In July of 1776 the Continental Congress met in Philadelphia to debate independence and voted to take action. Thomas Jefferson was given the task of drafting the Declaration of Independence with the approval of John Adams and Benjamin Franklin, who were the other committee members. The shot that was fired at Lexington that became known as the "shot heard round the world" paled in comparison to the words drafted by Mr. Jefferson that shook the world: "We hold these truths to be self-evident, that all men are created equal, that they are endowed by their Creator with certain unalienable Rights, that among these are Life, Liberty and the pursuit of Happiness."[39]

No country seeking its place in the world ever dared to proclaim that all men had equal rights and that they came from God, the Creator, and not the throne of a king or the seat of government power. Liberty was seen by these founders as a gift for all men to embrace and was not at the disposal of tyrants. This was indeed revolutionary. Freedom was tied to God. Faith in God was regarded as an essential part of the nation's foundation. The founders were hopeful they could build a new nation based on the rule of law and not the whims of kings. Their concept of law, like their concept of rights, was tied to God. This will be examined in more detail in Part 3 when the Constitution is studied. Christianity played a significant role in colonial America. It would continue to do so through the Revolutionary War and up to modern times.

2

Christianity and a New Nation

★

On July 4, 1776, John Hancock and fifty-five other patriots signed their names to the Declaration of Independence. This was not just a political action. These fifty-six men were identifying themselves as rebels against the Crown of England; they were putting their lives on the line, and many of them had much to lose. They were not a batch of malcontents or impetuous ruffians seeking to defy authority. They were men of prestige and in most cases wealth. They knew that if their quest for independence was thwarted by the British, they had just made themselves reservations for the gallows.

Why would these men of substance take such a great risk? They knew that the British military was the most powerful in the world and that the odds of success were against them, but still they signed the document. They signed not just because their hearts desired liberty, but also because they thought it was the will of Almighty God. The last sentence in the Declaration of Independence reads, "And for the support of this Declaration, with firm reliance on the protection of divine Providence, we mutually pledge to each other our Lives, our Fortunes and our sacred Honor."[1] This spiritual factor played a significant role in their desire to sign their names for independence. The words "with firm reliance on the protection of divine Providence" clearly reveal that these men believed that God was on their side and would be a source for their well-being and ultimate success. The words "sacred Honor" tell us that the bond they were making to the cause and to each other was solemn. This means they saw it as an action promised before God. It fits with the earlier proclamation in the document that rights are given by God that no man and no government can take away.

These audacious men did what in retrospect seems suicidal. They took their muskets off their mantels, weapons better suited for hunting varmints than going into battle, and they left their jobs as teachers, merchants, and even ministers to form a ragtag, volunteer army with the ambitious goal to unshackle themselves from tyranny by taking on the largest, the best-trained, the best-equipped, and for that matter, the best-DRESSED army in the world at that time!

The Hand of Providence

The fifty-six men did not see the spiritual aspect of their great endeavor as something to be slighted but were satisfied to give it prominence. They would trust in the hand of Providence to bless their efforts to wage war against the Redcoats; history gives account that this trust was well placed and did not disappoint. George Washington's words reveal this:

> I am sure that never was a people, who had more reason to acknowledge a Divine interposition in their affairs, than those of the United States; and I should be pained to believe that

they have forgotten that agency, which was so often manifested during our Revolution, or that they failed to consider the omnipotence of that God who is alone able to protect them.[2]

Washington fully believed that the help of God was a main factor in winning the Revolutionary War. He held a concern that the people might one day forget this divine assistance. In his "First Inaugural Address" Washington voiced his belief that God's intervention and aid were essential in the creation of the new independent nation:

> No people can be bound to acknowledge and adore the Invisible Hand which conducts the affairs of men more than the people of the United States. Every step by which they have advanced to the character of an independent nation seems to have been distinguished by some token of providential agency.[3]

Events throughout the course of the Revolutionary War reveal the invisible hand of God intervening on behalf of the American cause. In early March of 1776, General Howe, who commanded the British troops, planned to attack in Boston at night and had his troops at the ready, but he never led his men into battle, because an unstoppable force prevented him. That force was the weather. The previous day had been a pleasant spring day with warm temperatures. But at nightfall a raging storm suddenly struck with a mixture of hail, snow, and sleet and winds close to hurricane strength. Damage was sustained as fences were blown down and windows were shattered. One American lieutenant said it was the worst storm he'd ever experienced. The next morning, the strong wind continued as snow and sleet turned to a driving rain, making it impossible to fight. The British soldiers couldn't gain traction to ascend Dorchester Heights. They finally evacuated Boston without engaging the

Continental army. If good weather had continued, Washington's army would have likely sustained heavy losses, which might have doomed the success of the revolution.[4]

Some skeptics chalk up the rebel army's good fortune to simple luck. However, the Philistines in 1 Samuel 7:10–11 might have a different take.

The weather came to the aid of Washington and his men once again on August 29, 1776. They were trapped in Brooklyn and needed to escape the area or be routed by the British. They were outnumbered, poorly equipped, and low on supplies. To make matters worse, a cold rain was falling, making an escape from the enemy a difficult task. Then something happened that actually made the bad weather a blessing. The rain created conditions that produced a heavy fog so thick one could hardly see a man six feet away. Strangely, not all of New York had the fog cover. It was only in the area where the Brits needed to see what Washington was doing. The fog gave Washington the opportunity to get his nine thousand men over to Manhattan to fight another day.

One of the military battles that raised the morale of the American patriots and gave them confidence for future success was Washington's attack on the Hessians at Trenton. Weather played a role in that victory as well. In the middle of the night on Christmas Eve in 1776 Washington crossed the Delaware River when the Hessians were well into their Christmas celebration and had no fear of attack. They chose to hold mugs of ale instead of muskets, believing the snow and sleet would prevent an army from venturing an offense. Washington used the bad weather as cover to conceal a highly successful attack.[6]

First Ally

God's hand was evident in other ways than just the weather; He also touched the hearts of different people groups to ally with the Americans and their cause. One of these groups was the Oneida Nation. This Native American New York tribe played a very significant role in our nation's fight for independence. They served as warriors and scouts to help the Continentals fight against the British. It was a major sacrifice for them to do so, because it required them to break from their alliance with the six nations that were composed of the Oneidas, the Senecas, the Mohawks, the Onondagas, the Cayugas, and the Tuscaroras.[7] They were also referred to as the Iroquois Confederacy.

The Oneidas were the first sovereign nation to recognize the United States as a new nation.[8] They endured staggering losses in their commitment to fight with the Americans, but they made a very significant contribution. They were involved in the Battle of Saratoga, deemed the turning point of the war by many historians because this American victory persuaded the French to ally with the rebelling colonists, believing the revolution had a good chance to succeed.

An Indian tribe aligned with the Americans: where is the hand of God in this? you may ask. The Oneidas had something in common with the Americans seeking their freedom: faith in God. They had received the Christian faith from a missionary by the name of Rev. Samuel Kirkland, who is credited with being the key factor in the Oneidas siding with America. He came to work with the Oneidas in 1766 and spent the remainder of his life with them. He became their Christian spiritual leader as well as their advisor and mediator of disputes. He arranged for their schooling and for them to learn carpentering and the use of agricultural tools. Kirkland's missionary work was connected to a commission located in Boston where the patriot fires of freedom burned brightly. The British tried to persuade the Six Nations to ally with them by portraying the rebelling Americans as evil. The Oneidas could not accept this since they had received so much good from Kirkland and those associated with him. The Oneidas revealed that they valued their loyalty to the Christian faith as more important than their loyalty to the Iroquois Confederacy.[9] They chose to fight with the Americans. It could be argued that there might not be a United States of America nation if it were not for the Oneida Nation.

The French also came to the aid of the Americans. They played a key role in the final battle of the war at Yorktown, Virginia. British General Cornwallis decided to stay and face Washington there, hoping that reinforcements from General Clinton would arrive. If he set sail for New York, the French navy would likely intercept him. He left his fort and sought to cross the York River. This decision doomed his chances for victory as the Americans took the fort and he was prevented from crossing the river by a fierce storm. The French ships blocked any chance for reinforcements, so surrender became the only option for the British.[10] Again the weather played to the advantage of the Americans and the French. And once again Providence aided Washington's soldiers in this final battle.

Christianity in the Schools

After the war was won, the next step was to establish a government. Delegates from the states met in Philadelphia for a convention to address this task. The convention ran from May 25 to September 17 in

1787. The Constitution became law when New Hampshire ratified it on June 21, 1788, making it the principal document to guide the formation and operation of the government of the United States of America. One could argue that this was the real birthday of the nation, but fireworks still fill the sky on the fourth of July.

The founders did not feel that Providence ceased to be of help when the war ended. There were challenges and struggles in forming a new government, and they saw God's hand during this time. Talk show host Michael Medved documents this fact:

> The leaders who directed the military victories of the War for Independence viewed heavenly intervention as the key element in their success. But the political turmoil that inevitably followed their battlefield struggles produced benevolent results that contemporaries hailed as equally dependent on providential assistance.[11]

The third part of this book will focus on the Constitution, which was drafted at this convention in Philadelphia in 1787, and so the workings of Providence during this time will be studied in more detail in those chapters.

A few months after the Constitution was ratified, George Washington was sworn in as the first president, and the history of this new nation began in earnest. The evidence that this early history gives of the Christian faith being revered and influential on life and culture is profound. There is no better place to start than with the Bible.

During the war, Congress printed the Bible in America, since it was difficult or almost impossible to import copies. In 1782 the Continental

Congress approved what is known as the Aitken Bible, so named for Robert Aitken, publisher of the *Pennsylvania Magazine,* who requested the Bible be printed and used in schools. So the first English Bible printed in America became a reality. The front of the Bible contains the following statement: "Whereupon, Resolved, That the United States in Congress assembled . . . recommend this edition of the Bible to the inhabitants of the United States."[12]

This action by Congress was done prior to the adoption of the Constitution, but it is important to point out that it was not rescinded when the Constitution was the law of the land. It still was welcomed and used in the schools. The public schools in the early history of the nation provide strong evidence that Christianity was gladly embraced and regarded as useful in instructing moral values. In July of 1787, before the new Constitution was signed, Congress passed the Ordinance for the Government of the Territory of the United States, northwest of the Ohio River, which became known as the Northwest Ordinance. The purpose was to resolve controversies related to western expansion and make preparation for new states. Ohio became the first state from the Northwest Territory to be admitted, followed by Indiana, Illinois, Michigan, and Wisconsin. The ordinance contains a notable statement regarding education: "Religion, morality, and knowledge being necessary to good government and the happiness of mankind, schools and the means of education shall forever be encouraged."[13]

Schools were to be a high priority in the territory and for the states that emerged from it. Congress clearly desired religion and morality to be part of the education that these schools would provide. The Northwest Ordinance remained in place after the Constitution was adopted. The Supreme Court ruled it to be constitutional in a case called *Strader v.*

Graham in 1851. No challenge to religion and morality being taught in the public school systems was ever raised in the initial years after the Constitution was ratified and on through the 1800s. The words of the Founding Fathers leave no doubt that Christianity was a welcome influence in the education of the nation's children:

> [T]he Bible, when not read in schools, is seldom read in any subsequent period of life. . . . [It] should be read in our schools in preference to all other books from its containing the greatest portion of that kind of knowledge which is calculated to produce private and public temporal happiness.[14]
>
> Benjamin Rush, Signer of the Declaration

> Let divines and philosophers, statesmen and patriots unite their endeavors to renovate the age, by impressing the minds of men with the importance of educating their boys and girls, of inculcating in the minds of youth the fear and love of the Deity . . . in short of leading them in the study and practice of the exalted virtues of the Christian system.[15]
>
> Samuel Adams, Signer of the Declaration

> In my view, the Christian Religion is the most important and one of the first things in which all children, under a free government, ought to be instructed . . . no truth is more evident to my mind than that the Christian Religion must be the basis of any government intended to secure the rights and privileges of a free people.[16]
>
> Noah Webster, called the "Father of American Scholarship and Education," author of *A Compendious Dictionary of the English Language*

Reverence for the Bible and its use in schools was embraced by the founders, and Christianity was highly esteemed as an essential element in children's education. *The New England Primer*, which was widely used in colonial times, continued to be used as a textbook in schools when the colonies became an independent nation. By 1839 there were 450 adaptations completed by a number of publishers. The alphabet still used lessons tied to Bible stories and topics. Its Christian message was clearly evident in its pages, making it a textbook that was supportive of the Christian faith.[17]

This is significant because it stands in stark contrast to today's prevailing thinking that public education should be devoid of religion and that such policy was the original intent of the founders. If this were true and the founders wanted no religion taught, it would mean some forty years after the adoption of the Constitution, schools were in violation of the founders' desire to have the classroom totally secular. It would also mean that the founders allowed schools to be in violation by teaching religion, which was unlawful now that the Constitution was in play. The only logical explanation is that the founders did not want Christianity and its moral teachings to be expelled from the classroom. The continued practice of teaching Christianity in schools after the colonies became a nation happened because such was in line with the original intent of the founders, and those who would suggest otherwise are promoting a myth.

Christian Conscience Fills the Nation

The strength of Christianity in early America can be seen in the observation of a man named Alexis de Tocqueville, who came from

France in 1831 to observe how this new nation was faring under its republican form of democracy. He published his findings in his two-volume work entitled *Democracy in America*. This French historian and social philosopher was immediately impacted by the influence religion had on American citizens:

> Upon my arrival in the United States the religious aspect of the country was the first thing that struck my attention; and the longer I stayed there, the more I perceived the great political consequences resulting from this new state of things. In France I had almost always seen the spirit of religion and the spirit of freedom marching in opposite directions. But in America I found they were intimately united and that they reigned in common over the same country.[18]

Tocqueville was surprised to see how religion and liberty were seen as inseparable companions. He continued to expound on this topic in his book:

> Religion in America . . . must be regarded as the foremost of the political institutions of that country; for if it does not impart a taste for freedom, it facilitates the use of it. Indeed, it is in this same point of view that the inhabitants of the United States themselves look upon religious belief. I do not know whether all Americans have a sincere faith in their religion—for who can search the human heart?—But I am certain that they hold it to be indispensable to the maintenance of republican institutions. This opinion is not peculiar to a class of citizens or a party, but it belongs to the whole nation and to every rank of society.[19]

The power and reach of Christianity in America is documented by Tocqueville:

There is no country in the world where the Christian religion retains a greater influence over the souls of men than in America, and there can be no greater proof of its utility and of its conformity to human nature than that its influence is powerfully felt over the most enlightened and free nation of the earth.[20]

For this French historian, Christianity was the defining factor of the nation's character and identity. He believed it to be the most important element in the nation's success and that it would determine its future status:

I sought for the key to the greatness and genius of America in her harbors . . . ; in her fertile fields and boundless forests; in her rich mines and vast world commerce; in her public school system and institutions of learning. I sought for it in her democratic Congress and in her matchless Constitution. Not until I went into the churches of America and heard her pulpits flame with righteousness did I understand the secret of her genius and power. America is great because America is good, and if America ever ceases to be good, America will cease to be great.[21]

This foreign, independent observer looked at America in search of the determinants that were making it a great nation. He reported that he did not find its greatness in its fertile soil, its natural resources, its educational system, or its political format, including its Constitution. It was in its Christian faith that was proclaimed in its churches. In the words of Tocqueville, America was a good nation because of its faith, and if this goodness based on faith was ever ignored or neglected it would cease to be a great nation. This Frenchman gives a valuable insight into what America was like in its first fifty years of existence. It is a shame that most Americans are ignorant of this account of the early years of our country.

Tocqueville's tour of America took place during the waning years of the Second Great Awakening in America. Like the First Great Awakening, the Second Great Awakening had a profound effect on the nation. It featured two preachers and two denominations. The ministers were Lyman Beecher and Charles Finney, and the two denominations were the Methodists and the Baptists.

Two Preachers Changing the Nation

Lyman Beecher, the son of a blacksmith, became one of the most powerful voices for the Christian message during the time of the Second Great Awakening. This Yale alumnus pastored churches and held revivals where the combination of his physical vigor, sense of humor, and passionate conviction effectively moved the hearts of his listeners. After serving as a pastor in Connecticut and on Long Island, he pastored a church in Boston for six years then moved west to continue his ministry in Cincinnati.[22] Beecher was concerned not only about the souls of people but also about the social ills of the day. He founded reform movements and the organizations required to oversee them.[23] He was zealous in his opposition to alcohol and very active in the temperance cause. He pressed the Christian message during the time of the Second Great Awakening, which was important in curbing the advancement of Unitarianism, which was regarded as a heresy since it denied the existence of the Trinity and believed in the natural goodness of man.

Beecher's ministry would include serving as president of Lane Seminary in Ohio. He had thirteen children, two of whom became well known. His son Henry Ward Beecher became the successful pastor of a prominent church in Brooklyn, and his daughter Harriet Beecher Stowe was the famed novelist who wrote *Uncle Tom's Cabin*, which helped to fuel the Abolitionist movement against slavery.[24] (Christianity would play a vital role in the Abolitionist movement leading up to and during the Civil War.)

The second ministerial personality to make a major mark on the Second Great Awakening was Charles Finney. As a young man he had his sights set on a career in law, but at the age of twenty-nine he was born again in the small town of Adams, New York.[25] When he returned to the law firm, he told a potential client, "Deacon Barney, I have a retainer from the Lord Jesus to plead his cause, and cannot plead yours."[26]

Even though Finney held pastorates, his fame was tied to his role as a traveling evangelist. When he went to a town to preach, he did not always receive the warmest welcome from the local clergy. His preaching called for people to make a personal decision for Christ and not just passively wait for the grace of God to secure their salvation.[27] This was a bit of a challenge to the popular Reform theology advocated by those who were strong Calvinists. Finney also allowed women to have an active role in planning his meetings and sometimes allowed them to speak and pray in public.[28] This was innovative and not approved by all clergy, but it did give some momentum to the suffrage movement. The Broadway Tabernacle in New York City was built to house Finney's preaching, and it seated over three thousand people.[29] Finney later became a professor of theology at Oberlin College in Ohio and went on to become its president. He also was the main preacher at the First

Church in Oberlin, the largest building west of the Appalachians, for a number of years.[30]

Beecher and Finney were to the Second Great Awakening what Edwards and Whitefield were to the First Great Awakening. The Second Great Awakening was characterized by revival services that would last for weeks. The camp meeting became a popular method for evangelistic services. People would come and camp at a location for a week or more, as preachers voiced the need for salvation and the horrors of eternal damnation. These camp meetings attracted a large number of people. It has been reported that one topped twenty thousand people.[31] This method is still in use by some evangelical denominations today. The major result of this time of spiritual focus was the growth of churches as thousands of new Christians became active church members. In the early 1800s, the western part of New York was called the "burned-over district" because of the many revivals held in the region.[32] The "burned-over" reference was gleaned from the hellfire and brimstone preaching that was common in the revival sermons. There was a western expansion taking place in the country and the revival fires tracked to the frontier. Kentucky, Tennessee, and other parts west of the Appalachian Mountains felt the impact of this national spiritual awakening. Two denominations in particular benefited from this spiritual surge: the Methodists and the Baptists. The Methodists had a very organized means of outreach to the frontier. They sent out itinerant preachers called circuit riders who planted and ministered in new churches.

The Second Great Awaking not only changed the hearts and lives of thousands of people, but it also had an impact on the character and culture of the nation. It solidified the national moral conscience of the country. Christians became leaders in reform movements, which were known as antebellum reforms that focused on the use of alcohol, women's rights, and the abolition of salvery.[33] As people gained confidence in being involved in changing their lives through spiritual renewal, they applied that same boldness to participation in politics. They made moral issues items of concern to the workings of government. Enthusiastic Christians in local churches felt they could be the catalysts for change in law and the creation of institutions that would oversee change. They dared to be active change agents as temperance activists, antislavery advocates, and proponents of other variations of reform that would take their beliefs and effect political policy.[34]

The Evangelicals became a political factor in the wake of the Second Great Awakening, and they still are regarded as such today even if their impact has diminished. The Second Great Awakening brought about three significant changes:

- It pushed the idea of individual salvation and free will over predestination.

- It greatly increased the number of Christians both in New England and on the frontier.

- Revivals and public conversions became social events that continue to this day.[35]

The First Great Awaking was a positive factor in the successful fight for freedom as a new nation, and the Second Great Awakening was a key element in gaining the freedom of those trapped in slavery. The one atrocity that marred the founding and rise of the United States of America was slavery. It was a practice that was totally averse to the principle of freedom that was laid out in our founding documents. Many of the founders, including Benjamin Franklin, were abolitionists who knew that no victory would be won over Britain if the northern and southern colonies were not united. The newfound fervor of Christianity rekindled by the Second Great Awakening gave boldness to abolitionists and their movements.

Hudson, Ohio, a town not far from Cleveland, became one of the major centers for the abolition cause. Today the town still proudly displays brochures that provide information on the town's involvement in ending slavery. It was a town that enthusiastically served as a stop on the Underground Railroad as it helped runaway slaves escape to Canada. One of its leading residents who voiced opposition to slavery was Owen Brown, a wealthy cattle breeder and land speculator.[36] He was closely connected to the Free Congregational Church where he regularly spoke against slavery. Owen Brown's burning desire to end slavery reached one member of the Hudson community who would make a noted mark in the history of ending slavery in America. That one person was his own son, John Brown. He was the famous John Brown who would lead the ill-fated raid on Harpers Ferry, Virginia, that would heighten the tension that finally broke out into the Civil War. John Brown had heard many sermons on the evils of slavery. He finally decided to take action. He gathered twenty-one followers to compose his raiding party, and on October 16, 1859, they attacked the federal arsenal at Harpers Ferry.[37] Brown expected nearby slaves would join the fight on his side, assuring victory. That never happened and many of his men, including his sons, died in the fight. The man who led the forces that put down the skirmish was a colonel by the name of Robert E. Lee, who would later lead the Confederate Army. Brown was captured and hanged on December 2, 1859.[38] His actions were radical and violent, but some believed he hastened the start of the Civil War that eventually brought an end to slavery.

Not only did the churches support the abolitionist movement, but the famed evangelists of the Second Great Awakening fanned anti-slavery flames in their meetings. Finney proclaimed in his sermons that slavery was a moral sin, and wanted to see it terminated. He once said, "I had made up my mind on the question of slavery, and was exceedingly anxious to arouse public attention to the subject. In my prayers and preaching, I so often alluded to slavery, and denounced it."[39]

Lyman Beecher also took a strong stance against slavery and preached about its evils. As previously mentioned, his daughter Harriett Beecher Stowe wrote *Uncle Tom's Cabin*. When Harriet lived in Cincinnati, she met slaves trying to escape through the Underground Railroad. She wrote a series of short stories that revealed the horrors experienced by plantation slaves. At her sister-in-law's encouragement, she put the stories into a novel, which was published as a book in 1852. The book later became a play. The story of *Uncle Tom's Cabin* had a profound effect on people. It sold over 300,000 copies and persuaded many previously indifferent people in the North to support abolition efforts. The book sold even more copies in Great Britain and moved the populace to stand against slavery, such that Parliament, who would have welcomed a divided America, saw it as bad politics to support the Confederacy.[40] When President Lincoln met Mrs. Stowe, he said, "So you're the little woman who wrote the book that made this great war."[41]

Other Impacts of the Second Great Awakening

The Quakers were active in the Abolitionist movement. Roman Catholic priests encouraged their people to denounce slavery. Christian abolitionists in the North saw slavery not only as a social ill and scourge upon the nation, but also as a moral sin. Just as the British despised the "Black Robed Regiment" that proclaimed the virtues of liberty from their pulpits in the Revolutionary War, so the slaves of the South had this same regiment serving in their favor leading up to the Civil War.

The Second Awakening is also tied to the rise of the crusade for women's rights in America. Marjorie J. Spruill, professor of history at the University of South Carolina, writes, "Many women were inspired to become reformers, but were ridiculed for speaking out in public, and then started working for women's rights along with promoting temperance or opposing slavery."[42] The struggle for women's suffrage would be a long road, but the confidence to win that fight was forged in the revival meetings of the Second Great Awakening. It can be said that the Second Great Awakening was a booster shot for the American national moral conscience that helped to shape the country's culture, at least until a challenge was launched against it in the 1960s.

Christianity played a key role in the Civil War. Both sides claimed that Providence was on their side, but something remarkable took place among the soldiers who wore the blue uniforms of the North. They experienced a spiritual impact from a song. Julia Ward Howe wrote a poem that was put to the music of an existing song that became known as "The Battle Hymn of the Republic." She wrote the lyrics after visiting an army camp of Union soldiers near Washington, DC. The *Atlantic Monthly* paid her five dollars for it in 1862 and published it. "The Battle Hymn of the Republic" was the name given to the poem by James T. Field of the periodical.[43] The song was taught to the Union troops in many places by the chaplain of the 122nd Ohio Regiment. It has been reported that President Lincoln wept when he heard it.[44]

The fifth verse carries a profound message:

In the beauty of the lilies, Christ was born across the Sea, With a glory in His bosom that transfigures you and me; As He died to make men holy, let us die to make men free, While God is marching on.

The words "as He died to make men holy, let us die to make men free" are very sobering and carry the real purpose of the song. Every soldier that sang this song around a campfire had seen death on the battlefield and lived with the reality that he could meet the same fate. When they sang those words, they were saying that since Jesus died to make men holy through His atonement for sin on the cross, they would follow His example and be willing to die so those held in slavery could be free. They were willing to die for the freedom of people they never met and who were of a different race. This sacrifice needs to be commemorated by both whites and blacks in America. These soldiers saw their fight and possible death as a spiritual duty. The song has endured through the years as a Christian and patriotic song. It even appears in many church hymnals today.

A Christian Nation

The question is often raised, "Is the United States a Christian nation?" There are those who would line up to debate it, but for the founders and many of their descendants it was not a matter for debate. They accepted and even proclaimed that it is indeed a Christian nation. John Jay, the first chief justice of the Supreme Court and one of the authors of the

Federalists Papers, wrote, "Providence has given to our people the choice of their rulers, and it is the duty, as well as the privilege and interest, of our Christian nation to select and prefer Christians for their rulers."[45] John Jay saw no conflict in stating that America is a Christian nation. Would any Supreme Court justice today dare make such a claim? He wrote these words in 1816 to John Murry, some twenty-eight years after the Constitution was ratified. The Honorable Mr. Jay must not have been schooled on the separation of church and state concept that the liberal Left believes is embedded in the Constitution. A Supreme Court justice stating such things today would be subject to an impeachment!

Another Supreme Court justice saw America as a Christian nation. Joseph Story was appointed to the bench by President Madison in 1811 and served on the high court for thirty-four years. He wrote the prevailing opinion on a case in 1844 known as *Vidal v. Girard's Executors* that concerned a dispute over the $2 million that a man named Stephen Girard wished to be used to build a college bearing his name in Philadelphia. He willed the money to the city for that purpose but included a stipulation that no clergy were to visit or hold any post in the college. Girard's relatives tried to have the bequest ruled illegal because the restriction was averse to Christianity. Joseph voiced the beliefs of all the justices in the unanimous decision that allowed the bequest to go forward because it was believed that laymen could convey Christian teachings in the school. Joseph's opinion included the following words:

> Christianity . . . is not to be maliciously and openly reviled and blasphemed against, to the annoyance of believers or the injury of the public. . . . It is unnecessary for us, however, to consider the establishment of a school or college, for the propagation of

. . . Deism, or any other form of infidelity. Such a case is not to be presumed to exist in a Christian country. . . . Why may not laymen instruct in the general principles of Christianity as well as ecclesiastics . . . And we cannot overlook the blessings, which such [lay]men by their conduct, as well as their instructions, may, nay must, impart to their youthful pupils. Why may not the Bible, and especially the New Testament, without note or comment, be read and taught as a Divine Revelation in the [school]—its general precepts expounded, its evidences explained and its glorious principles of morality inculcated?[46]

In a Supreme Court case Justice Story actually designates America as a "Christian country." He went on to emphasize the importance of teaching Christianity to young people. It is not insignificant that the decision made by the court was unanimous. There was not one justice who disagreed with the claim that America was a Christian nation.

Forty-eight years later another Supreme Court decision echoed the sentiments of Joseph Story. The case was *Holy Trinity v. United States,* ruled on in 1892. A New York City church wanted to hire a minister from England but it was opposed by the government, which claimed that to do so would violate the then existing law that prohibited the hiring of foreigners. The court ruled in favor of the church unanimously and had Justice David Brewer write the opinion, which included the following words:

Our laws and our institutions must necessarily be based upon and embody the teachings of The Redeemer of mankind. It's impossible that it should be otherwise; and in this sense and to this extent our civilization and our institutions are emphatically Christian. . . . This is a religious people. This is historically true. From the discovery of this continent to the present hour, there is a single voice making this affirmation. . . . We find everywhere a clear recognition of the same truth. . . . These, and many other matters which might be noticed, add a volume of unofficial declarations to the mass of organic utterances that this is a Christian nation.[47]

Again, a Supreme Court justice declared America a Christian nation. A few years later Brewer provided more insight on his thinking on this concept, which reaffirmed his position. In 1905 he authored *The United States: A Christian Nation* in which he explained further:

But in what sense can it be called a Christian nation? Not in the sense that Christianity is the established religion or that people are in any matter compelled to support it. On the contrary, the Constitution specifically provides that "Congress shall make no law respecting an establishment of religion, or prohibiting the free exercise thereof." Neither is it Christian in the sense that all of its citizens are either in fact or name Christian. On the contrary, all religions have free scope within our borders. Numbers of our people profess other religions, and many reject all. Nor is it Christian in the sense that a profession of Christianity is a condition of holding office or otherwise engaging in public service, or essential to recognition either politically or socially. In fact, the government as a legal organization is independent of all religions. Nevertheless, we constantly speak of this republic as a Christian Nation—in fact, as the leading Christian Nation of the world. This popular use of the term certainly has significance. It is not a mere creation of the imagination. It is not a term of derision but has substantial basis—one which justifies its use.[48]

Brewer proclaimed America as "the leading Christian nation of the world." When he stated, in the opinion, that the country was a Christian nation, the other eight justices stood in unity with him. Years later a president referred to this case and Brewer's words to support the concept that America is a Christian nation. President Harry Truman wrote in a letter to the Pope in 1947: "This is a Christian Nation. More than a half century ago that declaration was written into the decrees of the highest court in this land [in an 1892 decision]."[49] A Democratic president told the Pope that America is indeed a Christian nation and referred to the *Holy Trinity v. United States* case. Why was there no outcry from those advocating separation of church and state against President Truman's words to the Pope?

In the Words of the Founders

The foundation for the concept that America was and is a Christian nation can be found in the words of some of the leading Founding Fathers. The following roll call of founders confirms this:

> The general Principles, on which the Fathers Achieved Independence, were the only Principles in which, that beautiful Assembly of young Gentlemen could Unite, and these Principles only could be intended by them in their Address, or by me in my Answer. And what were these general Principles? I answer, the general Principles of Christianity, in which all those Sects were United: And the general Principles of English and American

Liberty, in which all those young Men United, and which had United all Parties in America, in Majorities Sufficient to assert and maintain her Independence.[50]

John Adams

No people can be bound to acknowledge and adore the Invisible Hand which conducts the affairs of men more than the people of the United States. Every step by which they have advanced to the character of an independent nation seems to have been distinguished by some token of providential agency.[51]

George Washington

[Governments] could not give the rights essential to happiness. . . . We claim them from a higher source: from the King of kings, and Lord of all the earth.[52]

John Dickinson, signer of the Constitution

I do not believe that the Constitution was the offspring of inspiration, but I am as satisfied that it is as much the work of a Divine Providence as any of the miracles recorded in the Old and New Testament.[53]

Benjamin Rush, signer of the Declaration of Independence

He is the best friend to American liberty, who is most sincere and active in promoting true and undefiled religion, and who sets himself with the greatest firmness to bear down on profanity and immorality of every kind. Whoever is an avowed enemy of God, I scruple not to call him an enemy to his country.[54]

John Witherspoon, signer of the Declaration of Independence

Many others could join this list, but enough is conveyed in the words of these five patriots to provide evidence that America was founded as a Christian nation and that such was essential to its future success.

The Walls Cry Out

There is other evidence that the nation is strongly linked to Christianity, found in the memorials and buildings of our national capital. It is also present in our national motto and pledge to the flag. The Capitol Building has two paintings that positively support the Christian faith. One is *The Embarkation of the Pilgrims*, which portrays the Pilgrims observing a day of prayer and fasting led by William Brewster. The other is the *Baptism of Pocahontas*. If our nation was to be purely secular, then why would such artwork be allowed to hang in the Capitol Building?[55]

The Supreme Court building was dedicated in 1935, and even though some of the justices since then have rendered majority rulings unfavorable to Christianity, the imprint of this faith is on the building. There are numerous places in and on the Supreme Court Building that show religion was highly valued in the nation. The image of Moses with the Ten Commandments is carved into marble over the exterior east portico. The Ten Commandments are engraved over the chair of the chief justice. They are also present on the bronze doors of the Supreme Court itself.[56]

The Washington Monument is the tallest structure in Washington, DC. The capstone was placed on top of the monument in 1884. The east side of the capstone bears the Latin words *Laus Deo*, which means "Praise be to God."[57] This means that the first rays of sunlight fall on these words in the capital every day. The Christian linkage does not stop there. The cornerstone contains a holy Bible provided by the Bible

Society, along with a copy of the Declaration of Independence and the Constitution.[58]

The following quotation from Kerby Anderson, president of Probe Ministries International, reveals even more displays of the Christian faith in the monument:

> If you walk inside the monument you will see a memorial plaque from the Free Press Methodist-Episcopal Church. On the twelfth landing you will see a prayer offered by the city of Baltimore. On the twentieth landing you will see a memorial offered by Chinese Christians. There is also a presentation made by Sunday school children from New York and Philadelphia on the twenty-fourth landing.
>
> The monument is full of carved tribute blocks that say: Holiness to the Lord; Search the Scriptures; The memory of the just is blessed; May Heaven to this union continue its beneficence; In God We Trust; and Train up a child in the way he should go, and when he is old, he will not depart from it.[59]

It is amazing that one monument could contain so many connections to the Bible. The only reason why it would is that the people involved in its construction valued their faith and thought it was relevant to the nation's well-being.

The Lincoln Memorial was completed in 1922, and its walls bear words from President Lincoln's speeches. The left side of the memorial holds the Gettysburg Address with the words "We here highly resolve that these dead shall not have died in vain, that this nation, under God, shall have a new birth of freedom."[60] On the right side is his second inaugural address where God is mentioned fourteen times and the Bible is quoted twice.[61]

The Jefferson Memorial was dedicated in 1943 during World War II. There are four panels on the circular walls of the memorial containing Jefferson's quotes. The first three panels reveal that the third president gave high regard to God:

Panel One

We hold these truths to be self-evident: that all men are created equal, that they are endowed by their Creator with certain inalienable rights, among these are life, liberty, and the pursuit of happiness. . . . (The Declaration of Independence)

Panel Two

Almighty God hath created the mind free. All attempts to influence it by temporal punishments or burthens...are a departure from the plan of the Holy Author of our religion.... No man shall be compelled to frequent or support any religious worship or ministry or shall otherwise suffer on account of his religious opinions or belief, but all men shall be free to profess and by argument to maintain, their opinions in matters of religion....("A Bill for Establishing Religious Freedom," Section I)

Panel Three

God who gave us life gave us liberty. Can the liberties of a nation be secure when we have removed a conviction that these liberties are the gift of God? Indeed I tremble for my country when I reflect that God is just, that his justice cannot sleep forever. . . . (*A Summary View of the Rights of British America* by Thomas Jefferson[62]

Panel three is the most powerful as Jefferson showed concern that future generations might not see liberties as a gift from God and that such a belief might invoke the wrath of God upon the nation.

Our national motto and the pledge to the flag make room for the divine. The national motto is "In God We Trust." It appears on our currency and can be read behind the speaker's chair in the House of Representatives.

Francis Scott Key wrote the poem that contains the words that became our national anthem. The first verse is familiar and is heard at the beginning of ball games, but the fourth verse says, "And this be our motto: In God is our trust."[63] Written in 1814, these words first appeared on the two-cent coin in 1864 and have been on the one-cent coin since 1909. They graced the ten-cent coin in 1916 and were struck on all other coins since July of 1908.[64] It was not until 1956 that President Eisenhower signed the joint-congressional resolution making it the official motto of the nation.[65] This motto has so far endured efforts to have it replaced.

The Pledge of Allegiance contains the words "One Nation Under God." Congress passed a bill for these words to be added on Flag Day, June 14, 1954.[66] They have remained in the pledge even though they have been challenged in court.

It would seem fitting that a nation with such a rich Christian heritage from its founding forward would have the motto "In God

We Trust," and a pledge to its flag that would recognize the power of Providence. There are forces in our nation that do not embrace the nation's Christian heritage. They have employed sinister tactics to directly oppose Christianity in the public sector and elsewhere. We will examine them and their efforts in the next chapter.

3

Christianity in the Crosshairs

★

Christianity is under attack in the United States. The amount of evidence proving that this nation was founded as a Christian nation is astounding, but it has not deterred those who oppose this faith from unleashing their illogical and sinister attacks. The liberal Left has put the Christian faith in its crosshairs in order to decrease its influence on the life and culture of the nation. Why would anyone pursue such a course? The answer is easy: votes and political power. The Left knows that people who strongly embrace Christian values and seek to follow the Christian faith vote overwhelmingly for conservative candidates. The Left's thinking is, "Fewer Christians, fewer votes for conservatives." The statistics of the 2016 presidential election bear this out. Donald Trump received 81 percent of the evangelical vote while Hillary Clinton got 16 percent. This was a loss of five points from the 2012 election for Democrats.[1] According to the Pew Research Center, when church attendance was considered, the more a person attended church, the more likely he or she was to vote for Trump.[2]

The liberal Left, which controls the Democratic Party, seemingly cares about only one thing: power. Power is obtained by winning elections and controlling voting groups. When a voting group aligns with the opposition, then it is targeted by the Democrats. They seek to diminish and deplete the voting group's numbers. The Left went into full battle mode to this end in the 1960s and has carried the fight ever since. It took control of public education and secondary education systems where liberal professors far outnumber conservative ones. It gained more and more control of the culture as it dominated the entertainment industry and the news media. It is a shame that their strategies are working. The growth of Evangelicals is not keeping up with the nation's population growth. The liberal influence in public schools and on the college level has lured many Evangelicals from the faith. In 2003, 19 percent of people below thirty years of age professed "no religion." This number increased to 35 percent in 2017 when only 22 percent identified with any brand of Protestantism.[3]

Evangelicals packed a strong political force back in the 1980s when Reagan won the White House twice by substantial margins. Many credit the Evangelical vote as the difference that reelected George W. Bush in 2004, when many Christian voters took to the polls in Ohio to also vote to uphold Biblical marriage instead of same-sex marriage. The liberals in the Democratic Party have taken note of these political realities and have deepened their commitment to diminish the influence of Christianity throughout the nation. One tactic in their assault is the separation of church and state concept. It is as foundational to them as the founding documents are to the Republic.

Myth of the Separation of Church and State

The modern Left makes the case that the original intent of the founders was that we would be a purely secular nation where Christianity was to be expelled from the classroom, chased from the halls of government on all levels, and vanquished from the public square. The evidence in the preceding chapters clearly reveals that this was not the original intent of the founders. But the historical facts have not intimidated the Left one iota from launching their assault and proclaiming their bogus doctrine of separation from church and state. The Left has used slick marketing, the educational system, and a biased media to gain much ground for their cause. Their favorite weapon is the courts, where judges are appointed for life and never have to face the electorate. They believe they have found a loophole in our form of government to usurp the will of the people. Supreme Court decisions are almost impossible to change. What better way to advance your minority political views than to have activist liberal judges render decisions in line with their liberal positions rather than by precedence and the rule of law based on the Constitution. The use of the courts to substitute as a "super-legislature" is unconstitutional and has led to the dangerous doctrine of "judicial supremacy" by which Congress and the Executive Branch cower away from hard political decisions by allowing a liberal court to issue a ruling that is accepted as "THE LAW OF THE LAND!" But the courts can't make a law. They can only interpret those laws that Congress makes and the president signs. One would think that everyone who passed ninth grade civics would know that, but it's now accepted by most as the norm.

There are those who believe separation of church and state is in the Constitution. These words do not appear in the Constitution, nor is there a place where a case can easily be made for this concept. Where then does the Left obtain the basis for their doctrine of separation from church and state? They like to point to the "wall" between church and state, which they claim was set by the founders to prevent the church from having any influence in government or any place where government is in authority. This "wall" is not mentioned in the Constitution, but it is found in a letter by President Jefferson to the Danbury Baptists in Connecticut.

When Jefferson assumed office, he received a letter from the Danbury Baptists stating: "But sir, our constitution of government is not specific. . . . Therefore what religious privileges we enjoy (as a minor part of the State) we enjoy as favors granted, and not as inalienable rights."[4] The Constitution in the First Amendment declares "free exercise" of religion. The Danbury Baptists were asking for clarification because they feared it might be interpreted that the State (federal government) could change this free exercise of religion if it decided that this liberty was a right based on governmental policy. It is understandable why they felt this way, because Connecticut did have a state-supported church clear into the 1830s. In essence, this Christian group was asking, "Can the government intrude in our religious activity in the future?" They also had the concern that, as a minority denomination, they could be at a disadvantage if another denomination was chosen by the government as the national church. Clearly they were asking, "What reach does the government have into religion?" and not, "What restrictions are on religion regarding its involvement in public life and government activity?" They wanted to know what actions government could enact in their affairs, not how they were prevented from voicing their concerns in the political arena.

This distinction is significant, because today's liberals advocate for a strict separation of church and state and have used Jefferson's response to the Danbury Baptists' letter as the all-important document proving their belief, even though they actually flip-flop the concern of the letter.

The Baptists feared the intrusiveness of a strong government, whereas the secularists of the liberal Left want to turn the emphasis to exclusion of religious influence on government policy or activity.

Jefferson's response to the Baptists contains a phrase that stated his understanding of why the Constitution declared that Congress could not make a law that would establish a national religion, or any law that would prohibit the free exercise of religion. That phrase was "thus building a wall of separation between Church and State."[5] This one phrase, from a response to an inquiry letter—by itself hardly a heralded document on the scale of the Declaration of Independence or the Constitution—is what the Left hangs its mythical doctrine of "separation of church and state" on. They point to the "wall" Jefferson referred to as what must ever stand to prevent religion from touching any part of government and public policy. They have it all wrong! The "wall" in Jefferson's mind was not to prevent religion from touching government, but to prevent government from encroaching into a religion's activity!

The liberal Left chose one phrase from Jefferson's response and used it to launch a fabricated national policy. They discount the context in which the phrase appears. This is common practice for those of the Left; if something goes against their cause or even proves it wrong, they just ignore it.

Let's look at a larger portion of Jefferson's response, which provides the context and understanding that undermines the separation of church and state advocates:

> Gentlemen, The affectionate sentiments of esteem and approbation which you are so good as to express towards me on behalf of the Danbury Baptist Association, give me the

highest satisfaction. . . .

Believing with you that religion is a matter which lies solely between man and his God, that he owes account to none other for his faith or his worship, that legislative powers of government reach action only, and not opinions, I contemplate with sovereign reverence that act of the whole American people which declared that their legislature should "make no law respecting an establishment of religion or prohibiting the free exercise thereof," thus building a wall of separation between Church and State. Adhering to this expression of the supreme will of the nation in behalf of the rights of conscience, I shall see with sincere satisfaction the progress of those sentiments which tend to restore to man all his natural rights, convinced he has no natural right in opposition to his social duties.

I reciprocate your kind prayers for the protection and blessings of the common Father and Creator of man, and tender you for yourselves and your religious association, assurances of my high respect and esteem.

Jefferson used the words "natural rights." The Founding Fathers used that phrase to refer to unalienable rights, meaning rights that came from God and not from the State. This shows that Jefferson understood the Baptists' concern that government could one day pass a law that would infringe on their religious liberty. Jefferson was assuring them that this would not take place, because the Constitution prohibited the government from doing this. His wall protected religion from the State, not the other way around. It must be noted in his response that Jefferson paid tribute to "the common Father and Creator of man." This is evidence that he believed in God, who created man and the world, not that life came about by chance. Somehow the Left fails to point this out as it fervently misuses his words.

Jefferson himself poses a problem for the liberal separation crowd. He designated space in the rotunda of the University of Virginia for chapel services.[7] He welcomed religious organizations to locate adjacent to, and on the property of, the University of Virginia so that students could be involved in religious activities.[8] He supported the use of the Charlottesville courthouse for church services.[9]

In real-life practice, it does not appear that the Left's champion verifies their interpretation of his so-called separation clause. All these actions by Jefferson would be condemned by the liberal activists of today and outlawed by their willing black-robed accomplices. No president today could do what Jefferson did without the ACLU taking action and liberal politicians complaining on CNN. Jefferson's actions reveal that he welcomed religion as a valuable participant in civic affairs and did not see it as conflicting with the operations of the government. His words give more evidence, as he once wrote that religion was "deemed in other countries incompatible with good government, and yet proved by our experience to be its best support."[10]

He penned those words in a letter to Capt. John Thomas in 1807. Why haven't we heard about this letter, only about the letter from which the "separation-wall clause" was gleaned and its true meaning twisted? Why haven't Jefferson's many words in favor of the active role of religion in American public life emerged in this debate? Along with many other statements on the issue, Jefferson's letter to Capt. Thomas disproves the Left's claim that Jefferson supported anything like the separation of church and state as its advocates attest.

The First Amendment of the Constitution reads:

> Congress shall make no law respecting an establishment of religion, or prohibiting the free exercise thereof; or abridging the freedom of speech, or of the press; or the right of the people peaceably to assemble, and to petition the Government for a redress of grievances.

The amendment has the "establishment clause," which is "Congress shall make no law respecting an establishment of religion." What exactly was the intent of the framers when this clause became part of the amendment? This is the all-important question. Those who push the separation of church and state agenda claim it means all religious activity is to be void at government institutions, agencies, public events, and any other place where tax dollars are supportive. This position does not harmonize with history. We have already met Supreme Court Justice Joseph Story, who declared that America was a Christian nation in a unanimous court decision. In 1833 Story made a comment on the meaning of the First Amendment:

> The real object of the amendment was, not to countenance, much less to advance Mahometanism [Islam], or Judaism, or infidelity, by prostrating Christianity; but to exclude all rivalry among Christian sects, and to prevent any national ecclesiastical establishment, which should give to a hierarchy the exclusive patronage of the national government. It thus cut off the means of religious persecution, (the vice and pest of former ages,) and of the subversion of the rights of conscience in matters of religion, which had been trampled upon almost

from the days of the Apostles to the present age.[11]

Story is saying that the government of America would not designate one denomination as the official state church to be blessed with favoritism and political power. The amendment did not aim to diminish Christianity's influence, but only to make certain one denomination would not be favored over another. Many countries in Europe had official state churches, which resulted in persecutions and mistreatment of people who chose to align with a faith not part of the official state church. To avoid such treatment was the reason many migrated to America. The founders did not want to make the mistake of choosing a denomination to be the official church. For them, it was Christianity, yes, and official denomination, no.

Jefferson reaffirms Story's explanation of the establishment clause in a letter to fellow Declaration of Independence signer Benjamin Rush:

> The clause of the Constitution which, while it secured the freedom of the press, covered also the freedom of religion, had given to the clergy a very favorite hope of obtaining an establishment of a particular form of Christianity through the United States; and as every sect believes its own form the true one, every one, perhaps, hoped for his own, but especially the Episcopalians and Congregationalists. The returning good sense of our country threatens abortion to their hopes; and they believe that any portion of power confided to me, will be exerted in opposition to their schemes. And they believe rightly.[12]

Jefferson reveals that the purpose of the establishment clause was related to preventing one sect or denomination from being designated the official state church. Further evidence of this comes from George

Mason, who was known as the Father of the Bill of Rights. He recommended the following wording for the First Amendment: "All men have an equal, natural, and unalienable right to the free exercise of religion, according to the dictates of conscience; and that no particular sect or society of Christians ought to be favored or established by law in preference to others."[13] History provides clear proof that the original intent of the founders in the establishment clause was to prevent any one denomination from gaining official state church status, not preventing Christianity from having a public voice and a moral influence on the culture of the nation.

More Evidence Favoring Christianity

Some sixty-seven years after the drafting of the Constitution, in 1855, Congress presented a statement in a House Judiciary Committee report clearly showing that separation of church and state was neither a practiced policy nor something they even considered:

> At the time of the adoption of the Constitution and the amendments, the universal sentiment was that Christianity should be encouraged. . . . In this age there can be no substitute for Christianity. . . . That was the religion of the founders of the republic and they expected it to remain the religion of their descendants.[14]

The words "in this age there can be no substitute for Christianity" were proclaimed by Congress in the mid-1800s, which is clear evidence that a separation of church and state was never the original intent of the founders nor a belief held by those who followed them into leadership and power. This statement by Congress totally destroys the claims by the Left that America's founders wanted a purely secular nation devoid of any religious influence, especially from Christianity.

For the liberal Left, history poses only a minor obstacle for them. They just rewrite it, ignore it, and make sure that students are not taught the truth about it. The Left's thinking is, "Why worry about the evidence of history when you have the courts to turn to?" It is a tragedy that the liberal Left has taken the First Amendment and turned it into a loophole to advance their socialistic and morally bankrupt agenda. They have been able to get a majority on the Supreme Court to see things their way. Practices and freedoms that were enjoyed by the American people for more than 180 years have been erased. There is a long list of judgments handed down by courts in which they accepted the misinterpretation of the liberal Left on this issue of separation of church and state. Here are only a few:

> It is unconstitutional for students to start their school day with a nondenominational prayer. *Engel v. Vitale*, 1962[15]

> It is unconstitutional to require students to read the Bible in school. *Abington School District v. Schempp*, 1963[16]

> If a student prays over his lunch, it is unconstitutional for him to pray aloud. *Reed v. Van Hoven*, 1965[17]

> It is unconstitutional for a war memorial to be erected in the shape of a cross. *Lowe v. City of Eugene*, 1969[18]

> It is unconstitutional for a public cemetery to have a planter in the shape of a cross, for if someone were to view that cross, it could cause "emotional distress" and thus constitute an "injury-in-fact." *Warsaw v. Tehachapi*, 1990[19]

Even though the wording may be constitutionally acceptable, a bill becomes unconstitutional if the legislator who introduced the bill had a religious activity in his mind when it was authored. *Wallace v. Jaffree,* 1985[20]

It is unconstitutional for a classroom library to contain books that deal with Christianity or for a teacher to be seen with a personal copy of the Bible at school. *Roberts v. Madigan,* 1990[21]

Artwork may not be displayed in schools if it depicts something religious, even if that artwork is considered a historical classic. *Washegesic v. Bloomingdale Public Schools,* 1994[22]

It is unconstitutional for a kindergarten class to ask whose birthday is celebrated by Christmas. *Florey v. Sioux Falls School District,* 1980[23]

All of these items were acceptable at the adoption of the Constitution and many, many years afterwards. These court decisions are evidence that the Left has gained much ground in the culture war, and they did most of it without swaying public opinion or passing a single new law.

Not all judges on the high court have remained silent on this issue, even though they are on the minority side when it comes to public opinion. The late Chief Justice Rehnquist described the separation of church and state as a misleading metaphor:

> But the greatest injury of the "wall" notion is its mischievous diversion of judges from the actual intentions of the drafters of the Bill of Rights....The "wall of separation between church and State" is a metaphor based on bad history, a metaphor which has proved useless as a guide to judging. It should be frankly and explicitly abandoned.[24]

The words "mischievous diversion of judges" tell me that the late Chief Justice Rehnquist got it. He understood the true intent of the Founding Fathers, and it is ridiculous to wipe out 180 or more years of practices that were a vital part of our culture and rooted in our heritage. The Left has found the Achilles' heel of our republican representative form of government to be the judiciary. They have exploited it effectively to their advantage.

Jefferson again provides a problem for the separation-secularist crowd, even as they selectively take words from his response to the Danbury Baptists out of context in order to legitimize their position. Jefferson was not a fan of sweeping judicial power, a fact that is quite ironic since the courts have granted modern-day Leftists nearly all their victories. Not surprisingly, anti-religious activists fail to quote Jefferson when he speaks out about the judiciary system. Jefferson knew the dangers that the judiciary branch held when it was not accountable to an electorate, a point he strongly made in a letter to William Jarvis:

> You seem . . . to consider the judges as the ultimate arbiters of all constitutional questions; a very dangerous doctrine indeed, and one which would place us under the despotism of an oligarchy. Our judges are as honest as other men, and not more so. They have, with others, the same passions for party, for power, and the privilege of their corps. . . . And their power [is] the more dangerous as they are in office for life, and not responsible, as the other functionaries are, to the elective control. The Constitution has erected no such single tribunal.[25]

Jefferson's wisdom was not available to the framers of the Constitution when it was debated since he was serving as a diplomat in France at the time. It appears that his thinking was indeed missed. Jefferson points out the key reason the Left loves to use the courts. The judges are appointed for life and face no repudiation at the ballot box. The Left does not take their case to the legislature and go through the process for drafting a bill and having it passed then signed into law. This process is not advantageous to them, because their beliefs do not match the majority of the people. It is much easier for them to get a case before a court, often the Supreme Court, where the ruling becomes the law of the land. They make law via the court system rather than through Congress, which is an effective way to go when you seek to create laws against the will of the people.

Judges can make a decision that ignores history and precedence to advance their liberal agenda and have no fear of losing job security. Judges are appointed by presidents. Now you know why the Left was so infuriated when Donald Trump won the White House and the Republicans maintained control of the Senate. There was nothing the Left-leaning Democrats could do to stop the appointment of a conservative justice. They fear more such appointments could come.

The doctrine of separation of church and state, as the Left prescribes it, is absurd. To ascribe to their position you have to believe that the men who framed the Constitution immediately violated it by allowing the Bible and prayer in schools, Christian Christmas decorations on public property, and crosses to adorn the graves in government-owned cemeteries. You'd have to believe they weren't smart enough to know they were violating the Constitution they had created. That wisdom only emerged when liberal, activist judges became a majority on the court.

Agenda Advancement by Court

When Barack Obama ran for president, he said he wanted to transform the United States as a country. Basically, the Supreme Court has done that with its illogical rulings that run contrary to our nation's history and to the majority of the American people. The liberal Leftists that make up the modern Democratic Party are firm believers in "the ends justify the means," and they rejoice in their victories gained in sinister ways. The greatest jewel in their crown of victories via the Supreme Court is *Roe v. Wade*, which legalized abortion in every state. The people's representatives in Congress never got to debate the issue or vote on a bill. The Supreme Court became the lawmaker on this issue. Since most Christians stand on the side of life, the victory was all the sweeter for the liberal Left. A prime example of "judicial supremacy."

The Left does not stop at expelling all things Christian from the classroom, but also expends a great deal of effort inserting their agenda throughout the curriculum used by schools with the aid of the National Educational Association (NEA). Liberals willfully choose Darwin over Jesus. Evolution for a liberal is real proven science and should be taught in schools as the sole explanation for how life and the world began. A few years ago the town of Dover, Pennsylvania, wanted to add a course on Intelligent Design so that students could explore both sides of the debate of how life came to be. The Left sued and won on the basis that Intelligent Design was just a cover for creationism, which was tied to religion.[26]

Favoring Islam

Creationism is a religious teaching and therefore unconstitutional via court ruling. If enough Christian kids are pulled over to a belief in evolution, then there is a chance to win them over to the liberal political agenda when they are old enough to vote. Scripture does not endorse the gay lifestyle, but that does not prevent it from having a positive presence in the public school system paid for by the taxpayer. On July 15, 2011, Governor Jerry Brown of California signed a bill into law that required schools to teach students about the contributions of lesbian, gay, bisexual, and transgender Americans.[27] No word yet if the contributions of Christians will be taught.

Christianity may be snubbed, but not Islam. California once again led the way in a controversial education endeavor. A school had a textbook entitled *Across the Centuries*, which also came with Islam simulation materials. These materials were needed because the state legislature required three weeks of Islamic studies for seventh graders. I don't think Christianity or Judaism got their three weeks, but there was no opposition from the ACLU or other separation of church and state fanatics. The textbook presented the positive teachings of Islam and contrasted them with Christianity. I am sure that the horrors of the Moors' invasion, the Battle of Tours, and the execution of the Jews in Qurayza were left out to save ink.[28]

Students not only had to endure the textbook, but they also had to emulate being a Muslim. They had to take an Islamic name, pray in the name of Allah, simulate their own jihad (your guess is as good as mine on how they did this one), dress in Muslim clothes, memorize Islamic prayers, and fast at lunch during Ramadan.[29] This problem is not just in California. Tennessee also has pro-Muslim schools, as students in Williamson County have textbooks and materials that are pro-Islam and anti-Christian and anti-Jewish. Parents have voiced concern and are making a challenge.[30]

In Temecula, California, a charter school banned all Christian materials from its library.

A parent was appalled when she noticed the books that the librarians were removing from the shelves. One book was *The Hiding Place*, the story of Holocaust survivor Corrie ten Boom, who was a Christian in Holland and whose family helped to hide Jews during World War II until they themselves were captured. The Billy Graham Evangelistic Association produced a movie on ten Boom's story. When the parent voiced a protest, the staff told her that they had been given orders to remove all Christian books, books by Christian authors, and books by Christian publishers.[31]

The Pacific Justice Institute (PJI), a religious freedom litigation organization, took the case to represent the concerned parent. PJI informed the school superintendent that the school was in violation of the First Amendment by banning the books. Michael Peffer, the PJI attorney, sent the school a cease-and-desist letter "citing long-established Supreme Court precedent that strongly disapproves of school libraries removing books based on opposition to their content or message."[32]

Superintendent Kathleen Hermsmeyer ignored the appeal to the First Amendment and stated, "We . . . do not allow sectarian materials on our state-authorized lending shelves."[33] This made for some difficult situations, which were made apparent by the president of PJI, Brad Dacus, who stated:

> It is alarming that a school library would attempt to purge books from religious authors. Indeed, some of the greatest literature of Western Civilization comes from people of faith. Are they going to ban the sermons or speeches of the Rev. Dr. Martin

Luther King, Jr.? What about the Declaration of Independence that invokes the laws of nature and nature's God?[34]

Another incident happened in West Virginia when a parent showed up at a local school board meeting. The encounter can be seen in the documentary entitled *IndoctriNation*, which shows a father vehemently confronting the school board for assigning his daughter a book that could be described as literary pornography. He read a portion of the book, and the filmmaker had to bleep out many words because they were obscene. The Bible was not welcome at the school, but evidently literary porn was, and was even required reading.[35]

Indoctrination, not Education

Back to California to review an absolutely mind-boggling situation at a school in the San Francisco Bay Area that focused on one of the nation's founding documents. Fifth-grade teacher Steven Williams was prevented from passing out copies of the Declaration of Independence because it made a reference to God.[36] He also was prevented from using George Washington's Journal, John Adams' Diary, *The Rights of the Colonists* by Samuel Adams, and William Penn's *The Frame of Government of Pennsylvania*, all for the same reason, that there are references to God in these literary works.[37]

The governor of Louisiana wanted to use money from the 1996 Welfare Act to fund abstinence sex education programs for the purpose of lowering the teen pregnancy rate. The ACLU took action, claiming that abstinence programs were Christian-based and that to spend federal dollars on them would be illegal. The result was that a new source of funding had to be found.[38] The fact is that there are nonbelievers and some non-churchgoers who would welcome abstinence education in the school because they do not want their children sexually active while in school, for reasons that are not always related to a religious belief. Once again, the Left puts Christianity in the crosshairs of the public school system.

New York University psychology professor Paul Vitz did a study on sixty widely used school textbooks. He found that not one communicated the spirituality of the Pilgrims. He concluded in his study that textbooks were biased and practiced censorship to the benefit of a secular position and disregard for the truth.[39]

Public school is not the only educational environment that the Left patrols for advancing their agenda and taking Christianity down a peg or two. Tammy Bruce relates the case of a young man that endured extreme prejudice from a college professor. The student at Lakeland Community College near Cleveland was in a class where he was required to wear a pink triangle to symbolize homosexual pride. The student refused to do so, citing that it was contrary to his moral beliefs. He asked for an alternative assignment but the request was rejected. He was an honor student and was given an F grade for failing to participate. Never was there a time when the class had students wear a gold straight arrow for straight pride week. The student was in danger of being expelled until his story was covered by local television news. It created such a negative publicity problem for the college that the school caved and changed the student's grade[40]. What is so appalling about this incident is that this community college is supported by tax dollars.

The Bible stands for sexual purity and marriage between a man and a woman. This is not part of the Left's agenda. In their thinking, the

Christian faith deserves to be targeted in whatever way possible, because it will not change its doctrine when it comes to homosexuality.

Liberal Bias in Hollywood

The Left has another area where it has aimed its crosshair scope: the entertainment industry of film and television. They have declared open season on Christianity. Any derogatory action that can chastise and beleaguer the faith symbolized by the cross is considered acceptable. Tom Clancy wrote a novel entitled *The Sum of All Fears*, which was turned into a movie. The film producers made a significant change in the story. In the book the bad guys were Muslim extremists, but the Arab-American lobbyists prevailed on Paramount to make the villains in the film neo-Nazi European industrialists.[41]

Paramount did not want to offend the Muslim community by having Islamic culprits in the film even though Islamic terrorists were alive and well in the world. It makes all the more sense for them to do so since the Muslim voting bloc strongly favors the liberal Democrats. On the other hand, Hollywood did not have any problem with offending Christians when it produced the film *The Last Temptation of Christ*, which portrayed Jesus Christ as confused, weak, and bewildered. There were no worries about offending Jews in the film *King David*, which had David giving up his faith at the end of the movie, something not recorded in the Bible. These films were protested by Christians, but their protests had no effect on Hollywood. The films did not have much effect on the movie-going public either as they did poorly at the box office.

Hollywood was rocked by the success of the positive Christian film *The Passion of the Christ* by Mel Gibson, which chronicled the suffering, death, and resurrection of Jesus. The film was applauded by the Christian community, but it had to travel a difficult road to make it to the big screen. Mainstream Hollywood was not interested in the film. Why would they be? Jesus was not shown as corrupt or weak or denying His faith. No major studio would take on Gibson's film. Distributors did not line up to support it. Gibson finally decided to fund and direct the film himself. He eventually found a distributor, and the film made it to the theaters for a very successful run; it became one of the highest grossing films of all time.[42]

Some criticized the film as being anti-Semitic. They even went so far as to say that any film favorable to Christianity would be anti-Semitic by default. Hollywood did not worry about offending Jews with *King David*. These criticisms were a red herring, because the real reason Hollywood did not like the film was that it was pro-Christian. It bears mentioning that *The Passion of the Christ* lost out in the Academy Awards for Best Picture to *Million Dollar Baby*, a film that advocated assisted suicide.[43]

Christian apologist Ravi Zacharias said, "Television has been the single greatest shaper of emptiness."[44] The Left has used television to transfer this emptiness into the minds of Americans, especially the youth. Shows like *West Wing, Commander in Chief, Madam Secretary,* and *Homeland* have a liberal bias that is easy to recognize, but the small screen also takes shots at the values of the Christian faith and Christianity itself. Viacom's TV Land had a show, *Impastor*, set to air in July of 2018. The following quote describes this video debacle:

> TV Land calls their new program "Impastor" an irreverent new comedy. Christians are calling it disgusting! "Impastor" is a show set to air July 15 at 10:30 p.m. ET/9:30 p.m. CT that

includes a man stealing someone's identity who happens to be a pastor. The main character, posing as a gay preacher, recently hired sight unseen by a church that was aware of his lifestyle choice, but then started to notice other characteristics not typical of a pastor. The previews which air earlier in the evening are including the pastor having extensive knowledge of the quality of drugs and insinuating sexual relations with fruit such as cantaloupe. The church secretary catches the pastor sleeping around with women and other behaviors not typical of a Christian, much less a pastor.[45]

You can be sure that no one connected with this show is losing any sleep over the fact that what they are doing is offending Christians. The show *Friends* was a popular NBC sitcom that endorsed casual sex, homosexuality, and out-of-wedlock pregnancy—just the things you want your teenager to accept as normal behavior. NOT!

Will & Grace was a popular show in the earlier part of this century. It featured an attractive young lady with a homosexual male roommate. It advocated the gay lifestyle and always put in a positive light, undoubtedly to help convince heterosexuals to be more accepting of homosexuals and more sympathetic to their agenda and quest for legalized marriage. The Classic TV and Movie Hits website documents the success and impact of this show:

By 2005, *Will & Grace* had been nominated for 49 and won 12 Emmys. From 2001–2005, *Will & Grace* was the second highest rated comedy among adults 18–49, second only to NBC's own *Friends,* which usually preceded it on the Thursday night schedule. It has also been heralded as responsible for opening the door to a string of gay themed television programs such as *Queer Eye for the Straight Guy* and *Boy Meets Boy*. *Will & Grace* has won several GLAAD Media Awards for its fair and accurate representation of the gay community.[46]

It is little wonder that many millennials when surveyed now say they support same-sex marriage. Tyler Kingkade with the *Huffington Post* writes that 70 percent of adults born after 1981 approve of same-sex marriage, up 64 percent since 2012.[47] The strategy to use the entertainment industry to attack a Christian value and gain substantial ground has been very successful for the Left. Shows like *Sex in the City* have presented a lifestyle contrary to the Christian absolute of sexual purity before and after marriage. They undoubtedly have influenced women to experiment with more promiscuous sexual behavior.

The FCC has been a restraint on over-the-air networks' content to keep it from going too far in language and sexual scenes. Cable is a different ballgame. The FCC has no jurisdiction and Pandora's box has been opened. Soft porn films and shows are fair game, with vulgar language the norm. Christian values are clobbered by cable shows. Even though there are Christian cable channels, they have fewer viewers than the cable channels that feature R-rated programming

It is not just the shows that attack the values of Christianity, but also the commercials. Planned Parenthood once ran a TV commercial on MTV that took some heat for being too racy since it promoted the use of condoms for safe sex. The ad shows a young woman working with power tools and saying that her dad told her to always use the "right tool" for the job. Later, she is bursting into a bedroom where some guy waits under the covers. She quickly rips off her work clothes to reveal a

95

skimpy outfit and dives under the covers. Words communicate that the condom is the right tool to use when having sex.[48]

Another Planned Parenthood ad run on several Missouri TV stations zeroed in on birth control. A young girl and her boyfriend go to a Planned Parenthood center. Their marital status is not revealed, but everything indicates that they are not married. The couple is there to acquire birth control pills, and other young faces appear in the ad to voice their support.[49] These youth appear to be in high school. Planned Parenthood loves to have teens on birth control because they commonly forget to take their pill regularly and pregnancies happens. Planned Parenthood is more than happy to help with the abortions, for a price of course.

Could the Left now be turning their anti-Christian sentiments to social media? The National Religious Broadcasters (NRB) group has reported that some social media platforms are discriminating against Christian organizations. It states:

> New media platforms Facebook, Apple, Comcast, AT&T and Google have adopted policies to censor lawful viewpoints expressing Christian views or controversial ideas on "hot button issues." Some platforms, such as Apple's iTunes App Store and Google's search engine, have already started to use those policies to remove orthodox Christian viewpoints considered "offensive" or too controversial.[50]

Most likely if a Christian group presented any information stating their position on same-sex marriage or support for the pro-life movement it could receive scrutiny.

Just when you think the Left has gone too far, something else comes along that is both unbelievable and revealing. It is unbelievable because it is so extreme, and revealing because it shows the real sinister intent they have in opposing Christianity. On October 14, 2014, Todd Starnes of Fox News reported that Houston's lesbian mayor, Annise Parker, issued subpoenas demanding that a group of pastors turn over any sermons dealing with homosexuality, gender identity, or information about her. If ministers failed to do so, they could be held in contempt of court.[51]

Immediately the First Amendment comes to mind on two accounts. Do not the ministers have free speech? And, isn't it an encroachment on the religious exercise right that is also protected by the First Amendment? The mayor later withdrew her demand, but her actions do show how far the Left will go. What they cannot achieve now they may seek at a later time, if they feel public opinion is trending their way.

The homeschool movement is made up largely of Christians. The liberal Left is not a fan of this means of education. Of course they wouldn't be, because it keeps too many kids from being indoctrinated to the liberal agenda at taxpayers' expense. The Georgia Education Association, that state's version of the NEA, has sought to virtually end homeschooling in the state by trying to get a large number of requirements and restrictions placed on homeschools.[52] They have yet to fully succeed, but do not expect them to stop trying.

It is very sobering to get a glimpse of how far the Left will go in its attack on Christianity. Hillary Clinton gave us that picture in a speech at the 2015 Women in the World Summit when she said, "Deep-seated cultural codes, religious beliefs, and structural biases have to be changed."[53] She thinks religious beliefs have to change? This is not the responsibility of any government official, even a president. This is not the thinking of a candidate in a representative democracy; it is that of a tyrant. Tyranny is what we escaped from in the Revolutionary War. German philosopher G. W. F. Hegel, who was a young man in Europe at the time when the Constitution was being framed, penned two statements liberal Democrats would fully embrace:

> The State is the march of God through the World, its ground is the power of reason realizing itself as will. We must...worship the State as the manifestation of the Divine on Earth.[54]

Hegel saw the State or government as the replacement of God on earth. Any political leader ascribing to this concept would regard Christianity as foe, not friend.

As long as Evangelical Christians vote strongly for conservatives and Republicans, the liberal, leftist Democrats will continue to ridicule, harass, discriminate against, and directly attack Christians. This chapter has only scratched the surface of this issue. For a more detailed study, please refer to David Limbaugh's book *Persecution: How Liberals Are Waging War Against Christianity.* As the Left keeps their opposition alive against Christians, what can Christians do?

- Become more informed on the issues and seek out the real truth. A little tip: you won't find it on CNN or other so-called mainstream media outlets.

- Help pro-Christian candidates in their campaigns.

- Remember that who you vote for president matters for the long-term because presidents appoint judges. Leftist presidents and senators will put liberal activist judges on the court.

There is real power in having a conservative majority in the House and Senate. You may have to hold your nose sometimes and vote for a less than stellar candidate, but it is a better alternative than letting leftists have a majority, because then the attacks on the Christian faith will ramp up.

4

The Rise of Capitalism

★

You are a farmer. The light of dawn signals the start of a new day. You head for the field to harvest the crops. You are carrying a scythe, because that is what you will use to cut the wheat. The year is 1702 and there is no air-conditioned tractor or combine to ride over the field. You are destined for a day's hard work. It is the labor your father did and his father before him. You live in England and the land you work is not your own. It belongs to the lord of the manor. You are a simple peasant farmer like many others on the nobleman's estate. The life you lead is the one your sons will also experience. In your country, there are stations in life and few, if any, are able to move to a higher status. You are forced to be a tenant with little to no hope of being anything else. Any aspirations you have of rising to a higher station in life are quickly dispelled by those who stand above you.

If you lived in the town, you fared no better. You would likely be locked into a trade that was practiced by your father. Your prospects of accumulating wealth for a comfortable life would be dim at best. This was the economic system known as Feudalism. It was completely under the control of the crown. The king dispensed land to his nobles, who gave the king political security. The system definitely created a clear distinction between the "haves" and "have nots." The system was not just in operation in England but was common throughout Europe.

Capitalism Arrives in America

The vital commodity was land. Your wealth was defined by how much land you owned. If you had no land, you were resigned to poverty or subsistence existence. Land was needed to grow crops and feed livestock. Since the feudal system was strongly agrarian, it made land the prize to hold. Though feudalism secured the elite status of royalty and nobility, it did little to improve the lives of the common man whose population was increasing. The importance of land during this time is captured in the words of economist John Kenneth Galbraith:

> But no one could doubt the advantage of laying one's hands on an acre, or a hundred acres, or a thousand acres of fertile land. Nor could one doubt the deadly consequences of losing like amount. This meant that possession of land was strategic, and not even the philosophers whose ideas ushered in the Industrial Revolution could quite envisage a society where this was otherwise.[1]

Since most, if not all, of the land in Europe was spoken for, the expansion of wealth was limited. The scarcity of land made the search for more a matter of importance. This made the Americas, South Africa, and Australia attractive to Europeans.[2] Colonial America was seen as an entrepreneurial adventure by the wealthy man and the common man alike. Indeed, America gave the common man the opportunity to own his own land and carve out his own living on it. He might not own as many acres as the wealthy gentleman who chose the New World over less promising circumstances in his old country. The important thing was that he owned it and was now working for himself and not the lord of the manor.

The ships that brought the settlers to the colonies also carried an unseen passenger: the spirit of capitalism. This intangible factor cannot be underestimated. The hope of a better life that would materialize into real opportunity was an important motivation for people to say goodbye to friends and family members forever, and take a dangerous six-week voyage to an unknown new world. This world may have been unknown but it did have two advantages: land was plentiful and there was no established dominant social order that favored a noble class.

To gain a better understanding of capitalism, let's look at how it is defined:

> Capitalism: an economic system characterized by private or corporate ownership of capital goods, by investments that are determined by private decision, and by prices, production, and the distribution of goods that are determined mainly by competition in a free market.[3]

Given this definition, it will be beneficial to know how the free market is defined:

> Free market: an economic market or system in which prices are based on competition among private businesses and not controlled by a government.[4]

The important phrase here is "not controlled by a government." In the feudal system, there was heavy control by government and it was oppressive to the commoner. A new start in the New World of colonial

America had the expectation that this intrusive hand of government would not be as prevalent as it was in the old country. This ember of freedom that burned deep in the hearts of so many who made their way to America to seek a better life was passed on to their descendants. It would one day flame into the fires of the American Revolution.

Allan Meltzer reveals the prime positive aspects of capitalism when he says, "It is the only system that achieves both economic growth and individual freedom."[5] These two factors—economic growth and individual freedom—were nonexistent in the lives of ordinary people in Europe during colonial times, but the first ships carried them in the hearts of their passengers. If freedom was to be realized in commerce activity, it would only be a matter of time before it would be alive in politics. The winds that powered the rickety ships to America's colonial shores in the 1600s and 1700s also blew the zephyrs of liberty.

As we examine the economics of colonial America, it is appropriate to look at a system known as mercantilism, which holds the wealth of the nation as a top priority. The colonies were to be viewed as the tenants of the mother nation and were to increase her wealth. This became a point of contention between the thirteen colonies of America and the British Crown. An ocean between the two made it difficult for the heavy royal hand to keep the colonials under control, but it did not keep it from trying. The various taxation programs such as the Stamp Act and the tax on tea stirred up the anger of the American inhabitants, kindling the flames of liberty, and finally a revolution. The spirit of capitalism, which gained the spark of life in America, was not going to stand down for mercantilism.

We are all familiar with a document drafted in 1776, the Declaration of Independence, but few are as acquainted with an important book that was published in the same year. *The Wealth of Nations* by Adam Smith was written in Scotland. This visionary economist was a leading supporter of capitalism and his views greatly influenced the Founding Fathers. Smith believed that the main role of government was very limited. He saw it as having only the duties of providing for a national defense, the punishment of criminal acts, the protection of civil rights, and the provision of universal education. With a solid currency and free markets, individuals acting in their personal interests would generate profits that would enrich the nation as well.[6]

Alexander Hamilton, the first treasurer of the United States, supported the ideas of free trade and limited government. The latter concept he enthusiastically proclaimed in the *Federalist Papers* when he sought ratification for the newly drafted Constitution. In his *Report on Manufactures*, Hamilton presented many of the theories first advanced by Adam Smith, including the need to develop and cultivate the vast land available in America to create a wealth of capital through labor, the denial of inherited titles and nobility, and the creation of a strong military for national defense against foreign invasions.[7]

Smith and Hamilton both believed that as individuals gained wealth, the nation would also prosper. This is something that only happens with capitalism. America is the living proof of this. We have many rich people in our nation, and the common man resides in a middle class where he can provide for his family and enjoy discretionary income, which could only have been dreamed about by most some three hundred years ago. When a disaster hits in the world, America is the first to send aid. We send billions of dollars a year to underdeveloped nations. Our nation can do this because we are a wealthy country because of capitalism. No other economic system has this capability. Capitalism has lifted more people out of poverty than any economic system the world has ever seen. It began with those first ships that came to our shores.

Smith and Hamilton believed that limited government was a key to economic success. Government was to act like an impartial referee and not as an active player. Greed is not limited to people or corporations; it can also infect government. When government sees wealth being generated, wants to get its hands on it, whether through ownership (socialism), taxes, or regulations, and when government becomes an active player in the economy, it has a negative effect on the economy and is especially damaging to capitalism.

Pilgrims and a Printer

There are two examples of capitalism that reveal its positive impact on colonial America. One involves a group of people, and the other a well-known Founding Father. The Pilgrims came to Plymouth Rock in 1620. Their primary reason for migration was for religious freedom. They established a community and a system to transfer goods and services among its inhabitants. Their economic plan was not capitalism. The Pilgrims lacked the necessary funds for supplies and equipment to establish a colony, so they went to the Virginia Company of London and the Virginia Company of Plymouth for support. These companies were known as "adventures" formed to fund and equip colonial ventures.[8] The economic system established by the adventures was a version of socialism, as is confirmed by the following statement:

One of the key points of the contract between the Pilgrims and the Adventurers said that all colonists were to get their food, clothing, drink and provisions from the colony's "common stock and goods." In addition, during the first seven years, all profits earned by colonists would go into the "common stock" until they were divided.[9]

The "common stock" is a term linked to socialism. In essence, the Pilgrims had a socialistic commune and it did not work. William Bradford, the colony's governor, recorded that the socialist approach was an obstacle to the colony's growth. There were many complaints from those who were doing the majority of the work while others found excuses to not work hard but were not shy about partaking of the common stock for supplies. To avoid famine in 1623, the socialistic system was ended. Every family was given a parcel of land and the community became industrious. Those who were making excuses for not being able to work were now heading into the fields. The result was that three times the corn was planted. By the fall of 1624, the Pilgrims were able to export a boatload of corn and pay off the ventures that originally backed them.[10]

Socialism is the main competition of capitalism and is a cousin to communism. It sounds so noble: "from each according to their ability, to each according to their need." This utopia of equality is so wonderful, how could anyone be against it? The problem is that it does not work and has never worked, because it fails to account for fallen human nature. There will always be people who will try to get something for nothing. The people who do all the work and see others who do little or none will grow resentful. The question is, "Who decides who has ability and who has what need? How is the size of one's need decided?" In the reality of life, people don't just acquire things because of need, but also because of want. These wants can make life easier and more beneficial for one's family. Let's see how socialism is defined:

1: any of various economic and political theories and advocating collective ownership and administration of the means of production and distribution of goods

2a: a system of society or group living in which there is no private property

b: a system or condition of society in which the means of production are owned and controlled by the state.[11]

Socialism is characterized by "collective or government ownership and administration of the means of production and distribution of goods." It is for this reason that socialism is problematic. Government, or the few responsible for ownership, production, and distribution, can become corrupt, or at best, just plain inefficient. Either way, the end result is a disservice to the people in the system, and that is what the Pilgrims found out. Basically, the socialism experiment of the Pilgrims served them no better than feudalism, since the only equality it rendered was equal misery. When they embraced the capitalistic approach, there was surplus. The benefits of capitalism in comparison to socialism will be focused on in the next chapter.

Capitalism was best for the Pilgrims as a community, but it was also beneficial for the individual. An example of this can be found in one of America's most famous Founding Fathers, Benjamin Franklin. Back in the old country, it was common to follow in the footsteps of your father for your life's work. If your father was a cobbler, then you would make and repair shoes. If your dad made furniture, that would be your trade. America presented new opportunities. Benjamin Franklin's father was a candlemaker, which was a vital skill to have since there were no electric lights. But young Ben decided not to follow his father in this trade. After working in his brother's print shop, he believed more amiable circumstances awaited him elsewhere, so he went to Philadelphia in 1723.

He found work in the printing trade in less than stellar shops. He held other jobs but finally ended up back in the printing business. In 1728 he and a partner opened a print shop in Philadelphia that became successful. He was named Pennsylvania's official printer in 1730. His capitalistic interests go far beyond his operation of a profitable print shop. He once wrote a pamphlet entitled "A Modest Enquiry into The Nature and Necessity of a Paper Currency." This pamphlet advocated for an increase in the money supply to stimulate the economy.[12] It clearly revealed his support for capitalism, which he personally pursued in other business interests. Franklin was able to become a wealthy man through various businesses and real estate holdings. His wealth allowed him to turn the printing business over to his partner so he could give his attention to scientific interests. Franklin was a polymath, one who holds interest and expertise in many different fields. This word never found a better fit than in colonial America. Franklin embraced the freedom aspect of capitalism and he became an industrious inventor. He made the Franklin stove, which could be used for both cooking and heating a home more efficiently than the wall fireplace. People today still use Franklin stoves as an auxiliary heating source.

He improved spectacles by creating bifocals. His most heralded invention was the lightning rod, which gained him worldwide fame. Fires were always a serious threat in colonial times. Lightning strikes could cause a house or barn fire, and the ability to douse the flames was very limited indeed. This invention of Franklin's saved countless dollars in property and who knows how many lives.

Franklin's boost of the concept of American capitalism was on display years earlier in London when he was the representative for many colonies before the British government. One of the actions that riled colonial America and that negatively affected their commerce was the Stamp Act. It imposed a tax on all printed materials for commercial and legal use in the colonies. Franklin passionately denounced the act before the British Parliament and was able to get it repealed in 1766.[13]

Franklin also made a name for himself as a statesman, diplomat, and public servant. He was the first Post Master General of the colonies at the signing of the Declaration of Independence. He once even served as the governor of Pennsylvania. He is one of six people who signed both the Declaration of Independence and the Constitution. At eighty-one years of age, he was the oldest delegate at the Constitutional Convention. He enamored the French with his wit and charm during the American Revolution when he executed his diplomatic duties brilliantly in their country to secure them as an ally for America's rebellion against Great Britain.

This great patriot and Founding Father accomplished much in many fields. He was influential in establishing a library, a fire department, a hospital, and what is now the University of Pennsylvania, even though he himself never went to college. Not bad for the son of a candlemaker who would likely have been destined to ply the same trade if he had been born in England. Some historians call Franklin the first American because he voiced his desire for an independent nation early on in the debate. His love for free enterprise was no doubt the engine that moved him along this road. It is very fitting that this lover of capitalism has his image on the hundred-dollar bill.

In Step with Locke

One of the men who had a profound influence on the thinking of all the Founding Fathers was John Locke, an English philosopher and political theorist who was trained in the profession of medicine. His political views earned him the title "Father of Liberalism." Liberalism did not have the same connotation as it does today. In Locke's time it meant ideas tied to individual liberty for the people, not the tax-and-spend welfare state debacle that it has become in modern times. Locke lived for seventy-two years and died around the time Ben Franklin was born. Many think that his ideas helped to shape the content of the Declaration of Independence.

Locke certainly supported the concept of people giving consent to be governed by what entity would rule over them. This was not a popular idea with monarchies. It was one that the Founding Fathers supported as they declared themselves a free people and established a new nation. Locke's influence was not just political but also economic. His views on property and labor fit well with capitalism:

> [E]very man has a "property" in his own "person." This nobody has any right to but himself. The "labour" of his body and the "work" of his hands, we may say, are properly his. Whatsoever, then, he removes out of the state that Nature hath provided

and left it in, he hath mixed his labour with it, and joined to it something that is his own, and thereby makes it his property. It being by him removed from the common state Nature placed it in, it hath by this labour something annexed to it that excludes the common right of other men. For this "labour" being the unquestionable property of the labourer, no man but he can have a right to what that is once joined to, at least where there is enough, and as good left in common for others.[14]

He was stating that the work of a man's labor is his property. If he makes a house out of wood that he acquired lawfully from nature or wherever, the house is his property. A man who labors and is paid a wage, that wage is his property, which he can exchange for tangible goods or other services. Locke puts an emphasis on labor as a vital element in capitalism besides land. The early Americans were quite used to labor and land being a duet for the production of goods and services that would sustain life. A man owned land, but that land had to be cleared for farming by labor. The house had to be built by labor. The harvest by labor brought in the crops that would feed family and livestock. Land was property and labor was a means to property; and property could be and should be owned by the individual who had title to the land and whose hands provided the labor.

Benjamin Franklin was a laborer in various jobs that gave him the income to one day buy his own print shop and be a business owner. This has been repeated countless times in our nation's history. Capitalism can bless the labor as well as the business owner. This basic concept from Locke was treasured by the founders, who strongly believed in individual property ownership, which is a basic tenet of capitalism.

Those who came to the New World did so for religious freedom and for free enterprise. They wanted to gain wealth and own property, which were both unlikely if they remained in England. If you enjoy free choice in your worship and free choice in your economic pursuits, you are prone to want to have free choice in who governs you. You can see why Locke's ideology would be popular among the American colonies and especially with its leading citizens. The quest for liberty and freedom from the Crown of England was a natural third step for colonial Americans.

The Signers Make the Pledge

The Declaration of Independence included a list of grievances the Americans had against King George III. One of them reveals the disdain our founders had for needless meddling in American economic affairs: "He [the king] has erected a multitude of New Offices, and sent hither swarms of Officers to harass our people, and eat out their substance." The Americans felt they were being victimized by an unwarranted bureaucracy that was detrimental to their economic growth. The words "eat out their substance" are evidence that the colonials' private property was not being respected. The Crown wanted to be a major player and referee in the American economy. This was a major point of contention that helped our Founding Fathers choose independence. When they signed the Declaration of Independence, they did so under a solemn pledge: "And for the support of this Declaration, with firm reliance on the protection of divine Providence, we mutually pledge to each other our Lives, our Fortunes and our sacred Honor." They were putting their lives and fortunes on the line. Many of them indeed had fortunes that they had accumulated in free enterprise common to capitalism. Some lived up to the pledge. George Clymer of Pennsylvania had his home destroyed by British troops. Robert Morris spent one million dollars (not adjusted for inflation) of his own money to supply Washington's soldiers. Carter Braxton of Virginia gave silver and ships, many of which were lost. He died bankrupt. John Hart of New Jersey was driven from his farm, which was later destroyed by the enemy, and during his separation from his family, his wife died and their children were sent to live with neighbors.[15] The list goes on, providing ample evidence that these brave men lived up to the pledge. The departure from the feudal system to free market economies helped them make their fortunes, and they were willing to use those fortunes to establish a nation that would allow this economic freedom to continue. The American Revolution was a fight for liberty and freedom, but one must always remember one of those freedoms was the right to freely pursue your choice of work, own property, and gain wealth without the dictates of a king. The Revolutionary War was a fight to establish capitalism in the American colonies as much as anything.

Since capitalism became the economic system of the United States at its conception, it behooves us to understand the main characteristics related to it:

1. Free enterprise: Historically capitalism has been seen as two classes. One was the business owners who had the capital (land, money, or both) to start the business of their choice. The other class was the workers or laborers. The laborer actually could be considered a business himself since he sold his labor skills to the business owners who needed them. There was also a division of labor because some laborers gain more skills through experience and training, allowing them to demand

a higher wage. This results in more discretionary income, which has helped to establish a strong middle class in America.

2. Profit motive: When coauthor Steve Feazel took his first business class in pursuit of an MBA degree, the professor emphatically stated, "The purpose of a business is to increase the wealth of the owner." Businesses and corporations live to make a profit. This at first seems self-serving, but this is where the "invisible hand" of capitalism that Adam Smith wrote about comes into play. As the company produces, sells good, and makes a profit, those who buy the product benefit. The Ford Motor Company makes a car and sells it for a profit. The revenue from the car allows them to pay their employees, who now can buy goods to enhance their lives. The car sold then benefits the buyer, who now has reliable transportation to his work and also to travel to places of personal interest. The company's goal of profit to increase its own wealth results in benefits and in some cases helps others to gain a profit in their own ventures. The profit motive creates great incentive for people to take the risk of starting a business or developing a new product.

3. Minimal government intervention: It has already been alluded to that capitalism functions best when government has little involvement in the marketplace. Government has to be a referee in the economic process, but it must be careful not to overreach in this role or it will have a negative effect. This is the point of conflict today. Conservatives champion minimal government intervention, whereas liberals, who advocate a strong central government, want more federal control in the economy. Free market capitalists believe government should wear a striped shirt and make sure everyone plays by the rules, but when the referee starts wearing a team jersey and openly rooting for one to win

and another to lose, it's no longer a free or fair market.

4. Competition: A competitive marketplace is essential to capitalism. Competition is the key factor that allows the market to set the price. If there is no competition, monopolies will emerge and they will set the price. Government has used its referee powers to curtail monopolies detrimental to the public through legislation like the Sherman Anti-Trust Act and price fixing laws. Competition also has a self-policing action in capitalism. When the consumer has a number of choices about which like products to buy, he or she will switch from or avoid companies that become guilty of illegal practices or who lose credibility.

5. Willingness to change: Capitalism is a dynamic system. It is always adjusting to changes in the marketplace and to the environments in which it exists. The characteristics of profit motive and competition influence this change factor. There is always a desire to lower production costs that will increase profits. Improvement of a product or the introduction of a better product can give a company a competitive edge. Technology moves at a rapid pace. Some technological advancements have put an end to some businesses. The internal combustion engine in the automobile spelled goodbye to the horse-and-buggy business. The airplane replaced the train and ship as the major means of long-distance transportation for people. The Internet is having a major negative impact on print media; and email has cut sharply into stamp sales at the post office.[16]

The American Experiment

The nonexistence of nobility allowed capitalism to excel in America.

Americans won the Revolutionary War and their independence. Now its leaders were faced with the hard task of forming a government. There were those who would have by acclamation made George Washington king. Enough resistance to this idea prevailed so that a monarchy was not established, nor the favored nobility class. Alexander Hamilton wrote in *Federalists Paper Number 84*, "And of TITLES OF NOBILITY, to which we have no corresponding provisions in our constitution, are perhaps greater securities to liberty and republicanism than any it contains."[17]

If a monarchy had been established with a full-fledged aristocracy, freedom would have been greatly limited, if not completely destroyed. Instead, a representative republican form of government was created based on the Constitution. Our new government was termed "The American Experiment." Why did it receive such a name? Because no nation had ever been established like this. No royalty was put in place, the rights of the individual were to remain supreme, religious freedom was protected, and government was to have minimal intervention in commerce.

What the founders created was an economic petri dish for capitalism to grow in, which would make the United States one day the most powerful economic nation in the world. America was the first nation to have a green light to practice capitalism where the common, ordinary man could benefit from property ownership and the creation of wealth. The Americans claimed their rights from the hand of God, as was proclaimed in the Declaration of Independence. This made capitalism the natural choice for an economic system, since rights were not seen coming from a government, be it tyrannical or otherwise. Freedom and liberty were central to the creed of this new nation; therefore, it only made sense that its commerce would be conducted in free markets.

How this young nation fared with its experiment of liberty and free enterprise will be examined in the next chapter.

5

Free Markets for a Free People

★

The American experiment officially began on June 21, 1788, when New Hampshire became the ninth state to ratify the Constitution, making it an official governing document. Never before in history was a nation established with the rights of the common, ordinary man being the primary concern. Freedom made this new nation unique. One had the choice and freedom to worship. No one was obligated to support a national church. There was freedom to pursue wealth by any lawful means available. No established aristocracy bound a person to an economic station in life. The nation, with its capitalistic economy, allowed for anyone to move to the top of the economic ladder.

The Early Days

In America's early days, land was still the number-one prerequisite for generating wealth. The Revolutionary War left the United States hugely in debt to France. George Washington's first administration offered western land at one dollar an acre to help pay that debt. The land was cheap, but it had to be used or developed by those who purchased it. Much risk came with this great opportunity, but many took advantage of it and did well.

The new nation did not have large funds available to pay the soldiers that won its independence, so instead of cash, the soldiers were paid in grants of land.

Western expansion began to take place as many headed to the frontier for available land and a new life. Jefferson would double the size of the nation with the Louisiana Purchase. This purchase would boost western expansion, and control of the Mississippi River would allow for a valuable trade route to the port of New Orleans that would enhance economic growth.

Working the land would not be the only means for gaining wealth. Shipping on the rivers and high seas, milling crops and lumber, and skilled trades of quality craftsmanship allowed many to earn their living apart from the plow. Capitalism in the young nation emerged with America's first factory. In 1789 a British mechanic by the name of Samuel Slater came to America disguised as a farmer. He knew the guarded secrets of textile manufacturing in England, and he soon built a mill in Pawtucket, Rhode Island, with backing from two investors. His biggest problem was getting laborers since young men were reluctant to leave the farm, so he hired orphans and children. When Alexander Hamilton learned of the Slater textile factory, he enthusiastically praised it in his *Report of Manufacturers,* which listed the advantages of such ventures in America.[1]

Another textile empire was built in Lowell, Massachusetts, around the 1820s. The town was named after Francis Cabot Lowell, who, like Slater, built a mill based on his memory of what he saw in England. Unmarried women mostly filled the labor ranks at this factory. The water-powered mills were eventually replaced by the steam engine and the coal that powered it. This made the factories larger and more productive so more goods could be produced in a shorter time.[2]

The production of goods was an important capitalistic endeavor, but so was transporting them to various markets. Early on, canals were dug that allowed goods to travel more efficiently than over land. For many years, people dreamed of a canal that would connect the Hudson River with the Great Lakes. This would expand markets to the frontier and enhance the transporting people. Dewitt Clinton got New York State lawmakers to approve the canal, and construction started in 1817 and ended in 1825. Clinton's project was dubbed "Clinton's ditch" by his critics. The project was highly successful, bringing in $121 million on an investment of $7 million. Mr. Clinton silenced his critics and the Canal Era began in America.[3]

The Erie Canal had a great impact on the nation's economy and social environment, opening up the unsettled areas of Ohio, Indiana, and Illinois. The following quote reveals the effect the canal had on America:

> New York City became the principal gateway to the West and the financial center for the nation. The Erie Canal was also in part responsible for the creation of strong bonds between the new western territories and the northern states. Soon the flat lands of the west would be converted into large-scale grain farming. The Canal enabled the farmers to send their goods to New England. Subsistence farmers in the north were now less necessary. Many farmers left for jobs in the factories. The Erie Canal transformed America.[4]

By 1840 there were over three thousand miles of canals in operation, creating an inland water route from New York to New Orleans via canals and rivers. The high-pressure steam engine was invented in 1800, and when used to power water traffic it allowed for more rapid transport of goods. Cincinnati could now transport flour to New York by way of the man-made aqua highways.[5] The productive days of the canal system ended when a new innovation came on the scene, the railroad, which would further improve the moving of people and goods. This new form of transportation was well established by the 1860s when the Civil War clouds were forming. The railroad made location on a major waterway unnecessary. Towns so located could depend less on the slower transport by canals and rivers.

Emerging Capitalist Vanderbilt

More goods could be moved at a faster rate, enhancing capitalistic enterprises and inspiring more western expansion. The railroad also created wealthy capitalists among those who owned them. One such man was Cornelius Vanderbilt, who was born on New York's Staten Island in 1794. He followed in the trade of his father ferrying people and goods from Staten Island and Manhattan. He supplied outposts during the War of 1812, and following this conflict he operated shipping from Boston to Delaware Bay. This venture earned him the name "Commodore," which he relished. Vanderbilt University in Nashville bears his name and uses the commodore as its mascot.[6]

At the age of seventy, Vanderbilt turned his interest to railroads. He purchased the New York and Harlem Railroad and the Hudson Line, which ran along the Erie Canal, and then the New York Central Railroad. He later would control the railroad line from New York to Chicago.

As a businessman, he was known to be shrewd and innovative, which enhanced his wealth. When Vanderbilt died in 1877, his wealth was estimated to be $200 billion calculated on the nation's gross domestic product of that year. He was only outdone by Standard Oil cofounder John D. Rockefeller.[7]

The Vanderbilt story is a prime example of what capitalism created in America. Vanderbilt was not born of nobility. He learned the benefit of hard work from his father, who was not a rich man even though he operated a steady ferry business. The young Cornelius Vanderbilt saw opportunity and made the most of it. He did not despise the advent of new technology; he embraced it and transitioned from shipping via water to rail. His humble roots made him a bit out of place with the residents of higher society whom he would soon eclipse with his wealth. The likelihood of him obtaining the same success in England would not have been possible. His station of birth would have prohibited it.

Key Factors of Capitalism

Three factors make capitalism a powerful force in wealth creation and economic development. These three factors are incentive, innovation, and competition. One might ask, "What about profit?" Profit is not a factor, it is the purpose of each and all of the factors. The possibility of profit creates incentive. Those who engage in capitalism believe that their effort can pay off in gaining wealth and improving their lives.

People will go through the rigors of pursuing a college degree in order to have a profitable career. A person will risk opening a shop or small business to follow their passion and earn a respectful living. Individuals will invest time and money to create a prototype invention they hope will become a profitable product. All this creative energy powering capitalism is generated by motivated people, because they know that the economic system of capitalism can and will reward their success. This opportunity did not exist in the feudal system, and it is severely hampered in socialism and nonexistent in communism.

An example of someone who took the incentive to follow his passion and succeed is Rush Limbaugh. He had a radio career as a disc jockey that provided little job security. He did a stint with the Kansas City Royals but still believed he could make a difference if he could get back on the radio as a conservative talk show host. He got the opportunity in Sacramento, California. Some key investors liked what he was doing and believed it could go national. All the radio experts said that this experiment would fail because all radio is local. Rush proved them all wrong and not only became a multimillionaire but launched a new industry of conservative talk shows throughout the country. Coauthor Mike Huckabee, who started his own career in radio at the age of fourteen and now owns radio stations in three states, credits Limbaugh with saving AM radio as a medium and creating the influence of talk radio.

In countries with less freedom than the United States, Limbaugh's pursuits would not have been possible. They were possible in a nation that treasured freedom of speech and free markets. In 2020 President Trump honored Rush Limbaugh with the Presidential Medal of Freedom, paying homage to his influence and his example of innovation and entrepreneurship.

Very close to incentive is innovation. Innovation in technology, methods, marketing, and other areas distinguishes capitalism from other economic systems. There are new inventions, new improvements on existing products that make them better, and new procedures and modifications that help systems operate more effectively. The tyrannical governments of Europe in the 1700s supported the feudal system and provided no incentive for change and little benefit for new inventions. The American experiment in liberty, free markets of capitalism, and no aristocracy of nobility made the United States the real land of opportunity.

Inventions have propelled many common individuals from a low income to great wealth. These inventions have made life better for all who live in the nation and around the world. Alexander Graham Bell invented the telephone. As the phone lines became prevalent throughout the nation, the Morse code system became passé. What has transpired in the telecommunication industry is phenomenal. Today many people opt for only a mobile cell phone instead of a landline. The smart phone is more than just a phone. It also serves as a means for sending messages (texting), as well as sending and receiving emails, which replaces much paper "snail mail" and faxing. It also is a means for researching information via the Internet and taking pictures and making videos.

This is the spirit of capitalism. When an invention becomes established in society, it inspires others to improve on it, leading to better quality and, in many cases, lower prices. Texas Instruments introduced the electronic calculator in the early 1970s. The cost at that time was around four hundred dollars.[8] Nowadays the same calculating power can be purchased for four dollars at a supermarket checkout, or obtained for free as an app on your smart phone.

Many astonishing innovations that make us marvel, improve our lives, and delight our hearts have led to various unique inventions and industries. They would never have happened if it were not for capitalism. The incentive to acquire wealth motivates one to innovate and take the risk to present a new product or service in the marketplace. The free market society provides an environment for product improvement, which generates new products or better quality in a product. The result is that the consumer benefits.

One reason to pursue product improvement is to gain a competitive price. When Steve was in graduate school for his MBA, an economics professor made a very astute statement. He looked out over the class and said, "Remember this: price is powerful."

We have all made purchasing decisions based on price. Competitive pricing conveys another factor regarding capitalism: competition. The free market of capitalism allows for sellers of goods and services to set prices to attract customers. If one is able to innovate and produce an item more efficiently to reduce manufacturing costs, then the savings can be passed on to the consumer. The price is lower for the buyer and the profit margin is unchanged for the seller. Competition is vital to capitalism and it is not always tied to price. Quality, durability, enhanced customer service, and a host of other features can be in play in the competitive aspects of capitalism.

Often a customer is willing to pay more if the service is exceptional. A restaurant may have good food at a fair price, but if the service is poor, the customer will opt for an eatery where the price may be higher but the service friendlier and more efficient. In Steve's childhood, his family used to take vacation trips to Florida to visit his mother's relatives. There was never a motel where they lodged that provided a free breakfast. Today, this is standard for even a mid-priced motel. To be competitive in the travel lodging market, hotels and motels now feel the need to provide free breakfast service.

The most prominent example of gaining a competitive advantage in the area of service is Amazon. Using the Internet as an electronic catalog, the company started as the largest seller of books but has branched out into thousands of other products. If a customer can wait a day or so for a book or an item, then Amazon makes the shopping experience a non-hassle event. The customer can even read reviews of the item they are purchasing and make more informed buying decisions. Amazon is having an impact on brick-and-mortar stores. In fact, one large bookstore chain closed down in the wake of Amazon's success. Sears was once the leading retailer in America, but as this chapter is being written, it is closing stores and on the verge of shutting down completely. Sears started as a mail order catalog, but they failed to use the Internet as the digital catalog and Amazon seized the opportunity.

Competition regarding quality of product is paramount in capitalism. A prime example of this is the automotive industry. When oil prices shot up in the 1970s, consumers found themselves paying more at the gas pump. This provided an opportunity for Japanese auto makers to enter the American market with their smaller, fuel-efficient cars. They began to adjust to market conditions and offered luxury cars in the 1980s at a lower price with better features than their American competition.[9] The quality of the Japanese cars surpassed that of American-made autos and their sales soared. The high demand for the Japanese auto enticed the Asian manufacturers to build production

127

plants in the United States. Today 70 percent of the Japanese cars that are sold in America are made in America. One man said back in the late seventies that it was un-American for an American to buy an American-made car. What he was communicating was that buying an American-made car, which was of poorer quality than foreign-made cars, would only keep the American cars at low quality. His point was, when American car manufacturers lost market share because of their lower quality, they sought to make a car of better quality so they could compete with the foreign cars on the market. Competition motivates all competitors to constantly evaluate what other competitors are doing so they can keep pace, or they will find themselves no longer a viable choice by consumers.

From Average Grade Term Paper to Major Company

Three companies that have made tremendous impact on the nation highlight capitalism. The first company is FedEx. Frederick W. Smith came up with the idea for FedEx in a term paper when he was a student at Yale. He saw a problem that he believed was an opportunity for a company to take on the United Stated Postal Service. He revealed the logistical problems facing high-tech firms that needed electronic parts and other goods shipped to them quickly. Most air freight shippers, including the post office, used passenger air routes. This method proved to be unsatisfactory for urgent shipments. Smith conceived of a system that would be designed specifically for time-sensitive shipments. It would be ideal for medicine, computer parts, and electronics.[10] Today it is used for about any product you can imagine. Smith's idea was fantastic and revolutionized an industry. His professor was not so impressed since he only gave Smith an average grade. Smith first turned to a bank in Little

Rock, Arkansas, but was rejected because the banker thought it was an idea that would never work. Smith went to Memphis, found a visionary banker, and started FedEx there. I'll bet the banker in Little Rock hopes the world never finds out his name! But because of Frederick Smith, thousands of people are making more than an average wage.

Smith was operating an aviation sales company in 1971 that allowed him to see firsthand how difficult it was to get airfreight and packages to a destination in one or two days. He decided to put his term paper into action and Federal Express was born.[11] The company began operating on April 17, 1973, and delivered 186 packages to 25 cities. It quickly became the premier carrier of high-priority goods and set the standard for the express shipping industry.[12]

The company was a leading force in air cargo deregulation. Changes allowed FedEx to use larger aircraft, including wide-body planes like the Boeing 767. FedEx was a solidly established company by the 1980s and enjoyed a growth rate of 40 percent per year. It reached $1 billion in revenues in 1983, becoming the first American company to do so in ten years after its startup date without mergers or acquistions.[13]

It is very likely that everyone reading this book has been touched by FedEx. A panel truck or van has dropped off a package at your house or business, or you sent something to someone using this company. It is a service company. It does not manufacture any products to be sold in retail stores. Smith had an innovative idea that he believed would solve a problem and result in a profitable company. It was not without risk. It took two years for the company to become profitable. The expense of purchasing and maintaining aircraft, semi-tractor 18-wheelers, and smaller trucks would have been a daunting task.

Just think of what this company's service has meant to people. An essential part is overnighted to a manufacturer, keeping assembly line production downtime to a minimum and keeping workers on the job. A vital medicine arrives the next day, saving a life. A special item for the bride to wear at her wedding is found and able to be overnighted so she can wear it at the wedding and continue a long family tradition.

Frederick Smith became wealthy through his company, but he made many others wealthy also. Think of all the jobs the company has created: pilots, truck drivers, center workers, and administrative personnel. The company also likes to promote from within, giving workers opportunity to advance to better paying positions. The company is exemplary in its social responsibility actions. It is active in charities worldwide.

Some of the statistics related to FedEx are astounding. Their purple planes number 678, which is just about 100 fewer than United Airlines has in service. Unlike an airline, FedEx operates an extensive number of motor vehicles, numbering around 180,000. There are 450,000 employees at FedEx, and the company consistently ranks high as a good place to work. Each day, 15 million shipments are handled.[14] All in all, not a bad result from an average grade term paper, but such is the way of capitalism.

When It Comes to Capitalism, "Just Do It"

If I showed you a business logo similar to a check mark that is called a "swoosh," you would immediately recognize it belonged to the company known as Nike. The company was founded in 1964 as Blue Ribbon Sports. Phil Knight, a middle-distance runner at the University of Oregon, founded the company with his coach, Bill Bowerman. They had a desire to improve athletic performance through better footwear. They began as distributors of the Japanese shoe manufacturer Onitsuka Tiger (now known as Asics). The two's initial investment was twelve hundred dollars.[15]

The company adopted the name Nike in 1971, which comes from the name of the Greek goddess of victory. The trade name was revolutionized in the same year by, of all things, a waffle iron. One morning Bowerman's wife was making waffles for breakfast. Bowerman saw the grooved pattern of the waffle and thought that such a design would make a great sole on trainer shoes, helping runners get better traction on the track. The Nike Waffle Trainer became a reality in 1974.[16]

Capitalism also benefited the designer of the Nike swoosh logo. Carolyn Davidson, a student at Portland State University, created the logo and was paid thirty-five dollars (two hundred in today's dollars) but was later given stock in the company now worth over $640,000.[17]

Nike operates its own stores as well as makes their products available to other retail outlets. It currently sells more than shoes. Sports enthusiasts can find various kinds of apparel bearing the Nike swoosh, from T-shirts to full athletic uniforms. The University of Oregon's football team dons some of the most unique color combinations compliments of Nike. Today you can see the swoosh on sports equipment. It is not unusual to see the Nike logo prominently displayed on a baseball player's glove when the TV camera zooms in for a close-up. The company's largest store is not in America but is located in London, England. The store is 42,000 square feet and covers three floors.[18]

Nike entered an existing market of sports shoes. The founders were not introducing a new product but what they felt was a better product in an existing industry. To gain a sizeable market share they would have to excel in their marketing, and have they ever. Nike has not skimped on marketing expenditures. Purchasing television commercials on popular sports programs was wise and effective. Their slogan, "Just Do It," can be seen often on TV screens and on T-shirts.

The great impact of their marketing was and continues to be the use of endorsements by popular athletes. LeBron James receives an annual endorsement fee of $30 million. Kevin Durant gets $8 million. Golfer Rory McIlory receives $10 million, and Tiger Woods' deal nets him $20 million. The champion in the endorsement sweepstakes is Michael Jordan. He has not played competitive basketball in years, but Nike still pays him a staggering $60 million each year. If you asked these professional sport icons if they liked capitalism, I am sure they would respond with a resounding YES. Nike even benefits from team endorsements. It has a 15-year deal with Ohio State for $252 million.[19] Because of Nike, 73,100 people have a job, and this number will increase as the company grows. The revenue for 2020 is estimated to be $4.5 billion.[20]

From Dime Store to Mega Retail Company

One of the great stories of capitalism success is found in the retail giant Walmart. It is the corporation that many on the Left love to hate. Its only crime is being too successful. When the history of this retailer is examined, its humble start is apparent and one that many other retailers could have embarked on but chose not to. After a stint in the military, Sam Walton gained retail experience that led to him and his wife settling in Bentonville, Arkansas, where Sam opened a five-and-dime store downtown. The store became successful and inspired Sam to open his first Walmart in Rogers, Arkansas, in 1962 when he was forty-four years old.[21]

The success of Walmart can be linked to the principles Sam held. He believed retail success could be gained through offering lower prices while providing exceptional customer service, a concept not shared by many of his competitors. Sam Walton also believed that his store employees, or associates as he liked to refer to them, were a key to success. His beneficent focus on his associates topped anything in the retail industry. Sam outpaced his competitors with new ideas and innovative concepts. New store formats emerged, including the wholesale Sam's Club and the Walmart Supercenter. I am very familiar with the latter since it is a weekly destination for groceries and whatever other need might arise in our household.

Walmart became a publicly traded company in 1970, and the corporation became worldwide with acquisitions of chains in other countries or direct expansion. In 1992 President George H. W. Bush awarded Sam Walton the Presidential Medal of Freedom.[22] Highlights from the company's timeline history found on its website reveal the magnitude of the corporation that came from what many in my generation refer to as a "dime store":[23]

> **1972.** Walmart is listed on the New York Stock Exchange (WMT). With 51 stores, Walmart records sales of $78 million.
>
> **1980.** The Walton family establishes the Walton Family Foundation. Walmart reaches $1 billion in annual sales, faster than any other company at that time. Walmart has 276 stores and employs 21,000 associates.

1987. The company installs the largest private satellite communication system in the US, linking the company's operations through voice, data, and video communication.

1988. The first Walmart Supercenter opens in Washington, Missouri, combining general merchandise and a full-scale supermarket to provide one-stop shopping convenience.

1993. Walmart celebrates its first *$1 billion sales* week.

1997. The company celebrates its first $100 billion sales year.

2000. Walmart.com is founded, allowing US customers to shop online. Walmart employs more than 1.1 million associates in 3,989 stores and clubs worldwide.

2002. For the first time, Walmart tops the Fortune 500 ranking of America's largest companies.

2005. Walmart takes a leading role in disaster relief, contributing $18 million and 2,450 truckloads of supplies to victims of hurricanes Katrina and Rita.

2009. For the first time, Walmart exceeds $400 billion in annual sales.

2010. Walmart commits $2 billion through the end of 2015 to help end hunger in the United States. Walmart launches a global commitment to sustainable agriculture, aiming to strengthen local farmers and economies, while providing customers access to affordable, high-quality food.

2013. Walmart US announces it will hire any honorably discharged veteran within their first year off active duty.

Walmart projects hiring over 100,000 veterans in the next five years. Walmart commits to buying $250 billion in goods manufactured in the United States over the next 10 years.

2018. The company changes its legal name from Wal-Mart Stores, Inc. to Walmart Inc. Walmart announces plans to increase its starting wage rate for all US hourly associates to $11, expand maternity and parental leave benefits, and provide a one-time cash bonus for eligible associates. More than 1 million associates are expected to benefit from the combined wage and benefit changes.

One man had a simple vision for retailing and he took the risk to make it happen. The success has been phenomenal and millions of customers and employees have benefited. In his own words, "If we work together, we'll lower the cost of living for everyone . . . we'll give the world an opportunity to see what it's like to save and have a better life."[24]

Sam Walton proved the truth of the words of Steve's economics professor, "Price is powerful." The Walmart story is everything good about capitalism. The critics of Walmart gripe that it hurts local mom-and-pop stores in a community. Walmart itself emerged from such a store, which Sam Walton operated in Bentonville, Arkansas. How many mom-and-pop owners had more resources than Sam when he ventured into his first Walmart-type store? There were many, but they didn't have the idea or the fortitude to make it happen. A mom-and-pop owner in rural America has built one of the greatest companies our nation or the world has ever seen. It did not come from some New York City headquartered conglomerate. The success of Walmart is an example of how capitalism works and in the process benefits many people.

A debate was once held on the topic "Is Walmart good for America?" Besides the mom-and-pop store issue, critics wished to accuse the retailer of taking advantage of their employees, saying wages were too low and benefits not good or even avoided by using a large number of part-time workers. The debate cited the following favorable information about Walmart:

- Walmart saves a typical American family of four about $2500 a year. That's about what a family of four gets from the government in food stamps. That makes Walmart a major antipoverty force in the United States.

- Walmart is the single most important pipeline distributing wealth from rich countries to poor countries. Subsistence farmers earning about one dollar a day can take a low- or no-skill job in a factory making products for Walmart and afford electricity and running water for the first time. Walmart not only affects their living standard but their longevity as well.

- Since 1990, when Walmart became the world's largest retailer, the global rate of poverty has been cut by two-thirds. That's the sharpest decline in human poverty in all of history; more than one billion people have been lifted out of poverty during that period and Walmart is a major force in that effect.[25]

The writer covering the debate made an observation giving Walmart high praise: "It's hard to argue that anyone forces 100 million consumers a week to go to the store; they do it because, as Walmart advertising has said so many times—they save money."[26]

Mike remembers a time during a trip to Mexico when he was

governor of Arkansas. He and the minister of trade for Mexico were driving past a Walmart when the trade minister remarked, "Walmart has made it possible for our people to have the products they want at a price they can afford, and it's become the largest private company in the country in ten years."

The title of this chapter is "Free Market and Free People." Frederick Smith of FedEx, Bowerman and Knight of Nike, and Sam Walton of Walmart were living in the land of the free and were free to pursue their dreams and build companies that made them wealthy and at the same time blessed others. This is the way of capitalism. It is the best economic system the world has ever seen, but there are those who dare to oppose it, and sadly they live in this land of the free we call the United States of America.

6

Capitalism under Fire in America

★

More people have been lifted out of poverty by capitalism than any other economic system ever to appear in the history of the world. This is a proven fact and it is a primary reason why the United States is a super power that has blessed the rest of the world with its innovations and generosity when need has arisen. It is astounding that anyone within our great nation would want to seek to bring about the demise of capitalism, but they exist and are in places of power.

All economic systems are made by man and no man is perfect. Therefore, capitalism is not perfect, but that does not change the fact it is the best hope any man or woman has to honestly acquire wealth and improve his or her standard of living. Shortcomings in capitalism are far fewer than those in any other system vying to replace it. For a free people, only capitalism is the economic system that will complement and enhance that freedom. Rival economic systems supported by others, especially liberals, curtail freedom. At the heart of liberalism is big and intrusive government that seeks more and more control over the masses so its power can be maintained. This is an affront to freedom and a danger to capitalism.

Capitalism, by its link to freedom, is very dynamic. Its imperfections down through the years have been dealt with and improved because of its characteristics and the fortitude of those who believed in it. Our nation was founded to be a nation based on the rule of law. The people were to have input in making those laws through their representatives in Congress. Laws would be made that would properly protect the people from economic abuse by any who would misuse capitalism by exploiting others.

Laws Protecting People

There are some notable laws protecting the populace. The Sherman Anti-Trust Act of 1890 was the first significant piece of legislation to protect consumers from the dishonest acts of monopolies. What a trust is and how it operates is explained in the following statement:

A trust was an arrangement by which stockholders in several companies transferred their shares to a single set of trustees. In exchange, the stockholders received a certificate entitling them to a specified share of the consolidated earnings of the jointly managed companies. The trusts came to dominate a number of major industries, destroying competition. For example, on January 2, 1882, the Standard Oil Trust was formed. Attorney Samuel Dodd of Standard Oil first had the idea of a trust. A board of trustees was set up, and all the Standard properties were placed in its hands. Every stockholder received 20 trust certificates for each share of Standard Oil stock. All the profits of the component companies were sent to the nine trustees, who determined the dividends. The nine trustees elected the directors and officers of all the component companies. This

140

allowed the Standard Oil to function as a monopoly since the nine trustees ran all the component companies.[1]

The Sherman Act was named after Senator John Sherman of Ohio, who was chairman of the finance committee under President Hayes. It gave the federal government the right to bring legal charges against trusts in order to dissolve them. This law was designed to restore competition that would prevent price gouging. The consumer's best friend in capitalism is competition. Monopolies have no competition and can charge high prices to maximize profits at a ridiculous level. Companies seek market share, and one way to do this is to sell a product at a lower price than competing businesses. A monopoly is the only player in the market and holds 100 percent of the market share. Government has played its role as commerce referee at various times to end the unfair practice of a monopoly and reestablish competition in the marketplace.

Another practice that has the same effect as a monopoly is price fixing. A group of companies conspires together to fix prices for their benefit. They can fix a price at a lower level where they lose money for a time so they can drive a new company from the marketplace, or fix the price high to unfairly reap large profits. Both of these actions are illegal. The Federal Trade Commission is the agency dealing with price fixing. It seeks to maintain competition in the marketplace, but often, price fixing charges are hard to prove. A strong company may seek to buy out a weaker competitor, or two competitors may seek to merge and form one stronger company. These actions have to be approved to make sure that marketplace competition is not seriously compromised.

There are a few monopolies that are allowed to exist with the government's blessing. One is the United States Postal Service, better known as the post pffice. It is operated by the United States government. It has two monopolies related to it. One is the delivery of letters based on size and weight. This is why FedEx and UPS are allowed to compete with the postal service, because they deal with parcel packages, not letters. The other monopoly for the postal service is your mail box. Only the post office can place an item in it.[2]

The basis for this monopoly is derived from the Constitution in Article I, Section , Clause 7, which states "To establish Post Offices and post roads."[3] It might have been expedient to do this when America was a young nation and not many private companies had the resources or technology to successfully create and operate such a system. This is not the case today and there are many voices calling for the privatization of the postal service activities. Waste and debt are often cited as the reasons behind the need for this change. The Postal Clause does not deny competitors the opportunity to also create a delivery system. It just gives Congress the right to do it. It will be interesting to watch this play out.

Another area of legal monopoly is utilities. It would not be practical to have four different competitors running power lines in front of your house. Imagine how crazy it would be for repair teams to restore power after a storm. It would not make sense to have a number of natural gas lines buried in front of your property. Such an investment in infrastructure would make this impractical. What is in place is the designation of one company to provide power or gas to customers in a given area or region. There are government-run commissions that monitor these utility companies. If the company wishes to increase rates, they must make the request before the commission and provide justification. Here the government is entrusted with being the referee to protect the consumer and provide fairness in the distribution and sale of these energy products and services.

Patents are thought by some to be a means to a monopoly. This is not the case. A patent is a property right extended to an inventor for his or her invention. It has a life span of twenty years.[4] This gives the inventor the opportunity to gain wealth from his or her invention for a set number of years. The thought is that one deserves to be rewarded for the idea and the risk for creating something useful. It would be unfair to allow others to simply copy something that someone spent years of hard work and financial investment to create. The twenty years gives the inventor time to benefit from his or her creativity. At the same time, it puts a sunset on this advantage when others can enter the market and create competition. It should also be noted that when someone invents something, there is no guarantee that a market will exist for the invention. A new invention may improve something, but the existing alternatives may continue to be competitive, especially when price is a vital issue.

Overcoming Problems

Capitalism has had some less than stellar moments in American history. One was the abominable use of slavery as free labor to maximize profits. Our nation corrected this wrong at a great cost of life and resources, and the scar runs deep. Some companies allowed greed to motivate their practices and exploit workers. Child labor was used and many laborers worked ten to twelve hours, six days a week, with few benefits. These wrongs have also been corrected. The Fair

Labor Standards Act of 1938 ended the misuse of child labor.[5] In 1916 Congress passed the Adamson Act, which established an eight-hour workday for interstate railroad workers.[6] Ford Motor Company went to a forty-hour workweek on September 3, 1916.[7] Finally, on October 24, 1940, an amendment to the Fair Labor Standard Act established the workweek to forty hours for all companies as federal law.[8]

There are also the regulations set by the Occupational Safety and Health Act of 1970, which set up the Occupational Safety and Health Administration. There is some debate that this agency overreaches in its regulations, but history shows that America seeks to end exploitation of workers and protect them in the workplace.

Competition is vital to capitalism; and this is not only a benefit to the consumer but also to the worker. As the economy grows and more laborers are needed, companies have to compete against one another to attract qualified workers. It is therefore beneficial for a company to offer good wages, safe work environments, and benefits to attract and hold desirable workers. Managers are also finding that providing these things for employees increases productivity and lower employee turnaround. This enlightenment of management has resulted in saving companies money. Many companies are discovering that treating employees with dignity and benefits is a positive move for their bottom line because it results in employees having more favorable feelings for company management than unions.

There was a time when labor unions provided a needed service for the American worker, when many companies were bent on exploiting labor. In the course of time, unions, in many areas, became more of the problem than the solution. They became wealthy and powerful organizations and went in league with political forces. This was a perfect storm for corruption. The overreach of many unions cost jobs instead of improving them as many companies took operations overseas to improve profits. This was nothing more than the competition factor of capitalism at work. Competition doesn't just affect consumers, it also affects companies and workers, as is revealed in the following quote by Milton Friedman:

> So long as effective freedom of exchange is maintained, the central feature of the market organization of economic activity is that it prevents one person from interfering with another in respect of most of his activities. The consumer is protected from coercion by the seller because of the presence of other sellers with whom he can deal. The seller is protected from coercion by the consumer because of other consumers to whom he can sell. The employee is protected from coercion by the employer because other employers for whom he can work, and so on. And the market does this impersonally and without centralized authority.[9]

Friedman is describing the beauty of capitalism. Consumers can choose to buy from different sellers. This motivates sellers to compete to outdo one another to win a large share of customers. Sellers who may be passed over by some customers are free to find a market niche of other customers who can sustain their business. Workers are in essence sellers. They sell their service of labor. If one employer is unsatisfactory to their expectations, they are free to seek another employer who is. This environment of beneficial completion only works in a free society. Friedman's words "without centralized authority" are key.

When government seeks to go beyond its role as impartial referee and becomes an active player that seeks to influence market activity, this freedom factor in capitalism is threatened. This is what is happening in America today with liberal political forces.

Two Rivals

There are two rivals to capitalism today, socialism and communism. These two systems seek government control of economic factors. The two are advanced by their supporters as a solution to the undesirable trait in capitalism of companies exploiting workers for profit. Socialism and communism have a harder time gaining traction because many companies in capitalism have discovered that exploitation is counterproductive. Many companies pride themselves on the fact that they are considered a great place to work. This being true has not hindered those who advocate socialism or communism from pressing forward with their agendas. The two economic philosophies have some similarities:

- Each is built on the premise that individuals will contribute to society based on their own ability.

- Both advocate that institutions are centralized and controlled by either government or by collectives. This effectively removes private business as a producer of goods and services.

- Government (or some form of it) plays a large role in economic investment and planning, either in a centralized form or decentralized to local government bodies.[10]

The fact of government playing a large role in the economy is the main point of contention in relation capitalism. In socialism and communism, the government seeks to be a player as well as the referee in the economy. This creates numerous opportunities for corruption and gross unfairness in the nation's commercial transactions.

There are also some differences between socialism and communism:

- Communism views all property as being public property. Effectively, no personal property or items are held by individuals. Socialism sees individuals still having personal property but all industrial and production capacity would be communally owned and managed by consensus or government.

- Socialism is at its core an economic philosophy, whereas communism is economic and political in its requirement that government be the central owner and decision maker in all matters.

- Communism rejects any religion, and in a true communist state religion is effectively abolished. As socialism is economic only in its focus, freedom of religion is allowed, though some interpretations see it as promoting secularism in its nature (even if religion is not effectively banned).

- Communism sees the complete abolishment of class distinctions as everyone is effectively treated the same. Socialism sees a diminishment here but class distinctions would still exist as there is capacity for some to achieve more wealth than others.

- Communism sees the transition from capitalism as being

a violent revolution where the existing system is effectively destroyed as the workers rise up against the middle and upper classes. Socialism rather sees a gradual transition from capitalism through legal and political processes that see everyone essentially being treated equally at birth. People would still have the ability to excel and enter the equivalent of the middle class, but their children would have to work just as hard as they did to achieve the same.[11]

It is obvious that communism is the worst of the two. Communism is more radical in its establishment and operation. It strikes down private property ownership and makes government basically the only player in the game. It radically changes the political environment. Free markets are eliminated, and to maintain control, government must resort to force.

Socialism fares a little better, but is a very close cousin to communism. It advocates government as the dominant player in key areas, which is extremely detrimental to free markets. There is another way that socialism is more dangerous than communism. The radical positions of communism are easily recognized and quickly opposed. Socialism takes a more gradual approach that slowly establishes centralized governmental control. It may be less radical, but when it carries the day, it still has a negative influence on capitalism and economic growth. It chokes out the factors of incentive and competition, which are essential to capitalism's success.

Venezuela's recent experiment with socialism provides ample evidence this economic model is totally undesirable and can damage an economy and ruin a nation. This once emerging country has been decimated in the last twelve years. The country has rich oil reserves, which were nationalized by a socialistic dictator, and the "death spiral" of the nation began. The following facts give a somber picture of how bad things have become:

- The question of whether socialism can be an effective economic system was famously raised when Margaret Thatcher said of the British Labor Party, "I think they've made the biggest financial mess that any government's ever made in this country for a very long time, and Socialist governments traditionally do make a financial mess. They always run out of other people's money. It's quite a characteristic of them. They then start to nationalise everything."

- There are dire reports of people waiting in supermarket lines all day, only to discover that expected food deliveries never arrived and the shelves are empty.

- There are horrific tales of desperate people slaughtering zoo animals to provide their only meal of the day. Even household pets are targeted as a much-needed source for food.

- President Maduro is doubling down on the proven failed policies and philosophies of "Bolivarian Socialism," while diverting attention away from the crisis—pointing fingers at so-called enemies of Venezuela such as the United States and Saudi Arabia.

- A dozen eggs were last reported to cost $150, and the International Monetary Fund predicts that inflation in Venezuela will hit 720 percent this year.[12]

It is safe to say that the socialism experiment of Venezuela has been a complete failure. The tragedy of Venezuela's plight is the people who have had to endure the sufferings. Many Venezuelans are fleeing to Colombia. Samaritan's Purse, the humanitarian arm of the Billy Graham Evangelistic Association, is working with these refugees. It reports some unbelievable conditions that these people have had to endure. Six years ago, around 80 percent of Venezuela's households lived above poverty level, but today, 90 percent live below it.[13] A few pounds of rice could cost more than an average month's salary.[14] Reuters reported that in 2017 a Venezuelan lost an average of twenty-four pounds due to the food shortages and the impoverished conditions of the country.[15]

There is not one success story of socialism in history, but that does not stop politicians from continuing to recommend it as a replacement for capitalism. Why is this? The answer is quite simple: POWER. Liberal politicians desire to be in power and in control. People who are living successfully and pursuing their own dreams in a free market society are a bit hard to control, especially when they also have faith in God and own their own guns. People in this lifestyle are not dependent on government, so the liberal politician seeks to set policies as law that make people dependent on government.

The liberal politician does not regard socialism as a solution for economic woes so much as he or she sees it as a winning campaign strategy. Voters, uninformed of socialism's historic failure, are tantalized by its message of equality and provision of essential services, which are covered by government and are not the responsibility of the individual. It's Santa Claus in a business suit (or pantsuit) with a bag of progressive policies thought to be the answer to what ails the country. The way it often seems to work is, "If you want to get elected, run as a socialist. If you want to ruin a country, govern like one."

Socialism has crept into America and has increased its pace to a brisk walk. Let's look at a couple of examples. Our first focus is on Social Security. The Democrats back in FDR's day decided the federal government should go into the preparation-for-retirement business. The Federal Insurance Contributions Act (FICA) is a tax the vast majority of the working population pays to cover Social Security and Medicare. What an employee pays is also matched by an employer. When an employee reaches a certain age, he or she can sign up to collect Social Security payments, and when sixty-five years of age is reached then they are eligible for Medicare.

On the surface, this all sounds so noble and benevolent. Our federal government is watching out for us. It wants us to have income during our golden retirement years. I did some calculations, as have others. If either of us had taken what we paid into Social Security and invested in a diversified retirement program with a conservative approach, we would have gotten three to four times more dollars than what we now will be receiving in Social Security. Some would say that we might not have been consistent in making the payments to a retirement fund. Our response is, WE have that responsibility. The government should not have the right to tell us to buy an inferior retirement plan. We are responsible for our own future. Planning and preparing for retirement is a personal responsibility, not the government's. The government decided to be a player in the retirement industry and, by also being the referee, made the rule that everyone working in most places would have to buy their product. Major market share gained with no marketing expense.

Social Security has another downside. It goes away at death. If I have assets in my personal retirement fund or program, when I die, they can be passed on to my heirs. If a person who pays into Social Security for years and tragically passes away at age sixty, his or her family gets no Social Security payments. It just is a windfall for the government. This means one is worth more to the government dead than alive. This being true, does anyone want the government handling our health care? It sounds like a conflict of interest.

Social Security funds paid by employers and employees do not go into an escrow fund where they can generate growth. Instead, they go into the general fund where politicians from both parties use them for "pork barrel" projects to help their own political careers.

One would think that even with its imperfections, Social Security is a worthy program that does help retired people. It may come as a surprise to you to learn that its primary purpose is about more than helping people to retire comfortably. One of its main purposes is to get and keep politicians elected. Politicians are about power. They get power by winning elections. Their strategy for winning elections is to compose a coalition of voting blocs that are dependent on or loyal to them. Senior citizens are a coveted voting bloc. If a number of them can be made dependent on big government, then they will likely vote for the party who advocated the program on which they were dependent. Election after election, Democratic candidates have told voters that if they elect Republicans, it would likely be the end of Social Security. Such ridiculous claims put fear into even conservative senior citizens. Republicans have won elections and they have not touched Social

Security, so the fearmongering by Democrats on this issue has lost its impact. In the 2016 election, Trump won the fifty-plus vote, taking 53 percent of it.

Healthcare, Beware

Liberals have moved on to a more encompassing issue: healthcare. Liberal Democrats marvel at social healthcare systems in Europe and in Canada. If they could install such a system in America, it would be the crowning jewel in their quest for dependency on big government. A major effort was tried in the passing of the Affordable Healthcare Act, more commonly known as Obamacare. That is a better name for it, since it did not create affordable healthcare. Instead, a vast number of Americans saw their healthcare costs rise significantly. They also found the promise "You can keep your doctor and you can keep your healthcare insurance plan" was erroneous. Obamacare was disastrous and led to Republicans making great gains in the next mid-term elections.

However, this has not deterred liberals from pressing forward for socialized medicine and a one-payer system for healthcare. If Social Security could capture the bloc of senior citizens into dependency, how much better would it be to have an entire nation dependent on government through socialized medicine? Democrats see government-run healthcare as a security blanket to power. Never mind that such care would be inferior to present-day care. Never mind that it would result in rationing care to the elderly. Never mind that people will have to wait longer to get the care they need. If it can secure their power, all will be worth it. At every election, Democrats say, "A vote for Republicans is a vote to end your healthcare."

The Democrats want the federal government to have a monopoly in running the healthcare industry. Goodbye incentive to create new medicines and new procedures, and to bring smart minds into the healthcare field. Goodbye competition in access to services. The federal government already runs a healthcare system known as the VA. The reports on its administration of this system are extremely poor. Veterans have reported waiting a long time to get care that is often substandard. The federal government has no business running the healthcare business as a monopoly and pulling it from the free market environment.

The Green Scheme

What is concerning about socialism, which liberals are advancing in America today, is its trend to embrace communistic characteristics. At the writing of this book, freshman congresswoman Alexandria Ocasio-Cortez of New York introduced her Green New Deal bill, which many of the 2020 presidential contenders on the Democratic side supported. The deal calls for 100 percent of America's power to be met by clean, renewable, and zero-emission energy sources. The ultimate goal is to end the use of fossil fuels completely.[16] The content of the bill includes the following goals:

- "Upgrading all existing buildings" in the country for energy efficiency

- Working with farmers "to eliminate pollution and greenhouse gas emissions . . . as much as is technologically feasible" (while supporting family farms and promoting "universal access to healthy food")

- "Overhauling transportation systems" to reduce emissions—

including expanding electric car manufacturing, building "charging stations everywhere," and expanding high-speed rail to "a scale where air travel stops becoming necessary"

- A guaranteed job "with a family-sustaining wage, adequate family and medical leave, paid vacations and retirement security" for every American

- "High-quality health care" for all Americans[17]

The bill, if it became law, would want all of this to be accomplished in ten years. To upgrade all buildings in the country to be powered by sources other than fossils fuels in this time frame is ridiculous. Both authors have worked in state government jobs and learned that government moves at the speed of dark. The "working with farmers to eliminate pollution" is in reference to reducing, if not ending, bovine flatulence—cows farting. I guess the beef industry would have to go the way of the rotary dial phone. Making air travel unnecessary would be the end of airlines. This would make it a bit difficult to get to Hawaii and Europe. High-speed rail on these trips would get you a little wet. Ships going to these destinations would replace hours of travel time with days of travel time. These ships would have to surrender their diesel fuel for solar panels . . . or maybe we bring back sails.

The guaranteed job proposal has been extended to people unwilling to work. One could receive a paycheck without even going to work. How does a paid vacation work for someone who is getting a salary for not working because they don't want to work? There is also high-quality healthcare promised for all Americans. High quality is not something that is delivered by a monopoly, especially one run by the government. The expanded role of government in this deal is enormous; its negative effect on capitalism and free markets would be devastating. A loyal Marxist could not have done a better job at creating an instrument to move the nation closer to communism. One of the means for funding this economic disaster in the making is to cut the military budget by 50 percent. Not only would the Green New Deal end capitalism in America, it would also threaten our national security by weakening our military.[18] China and India are the two biggest polluter nations in the world, but the New Green Deal does not make any statements mentioning them and their need to also comply with the goals of this proposed legislation.

The Green New Deal reveals how actively the radical environmentalists are involved in opposing capitalism. One of the sacred cows of liberalism is global warming, which had to be renamed climate change because too many cold spells were detrimental to the term "global warming." John Eidson, a 1968 electrical engineer graduate of Georgia Tech, wrote a most insightful article in the *American Thinker* that exposes the real objective of climate change. In the article, he cites a quote from Christiana Figueres, who was at the time executive secretary of the UN's Framework Convention on Climate Change:

> This is the first time in human history that we are setting ourselves the task of intentionally changing [getting rid of] the economic development model that has reigned since the Industrial Revolution.[19]

These words were spoken at a press conference in Brussels in February 2015. The economic development model is none other than capitalism. A year earlier this same lady complained that America's two-party constitutional system was hindering the UN's climate objectives.

She went on to express the one-party system of Communism as found in China would be a better choice for America if environmental goals are to be achieved[20]. Climate change is the Trojan horse for advancing communism in America. It is alarming how many in our nation are falling for it.

Figueres does not stand alone in her thinking. Dr. Ottmar Edenhofer, a senior UN official and co-chair of the UN IPCC's Working Group III, makes comments that leave no doubt what the real goal of climate change is. He made the following statement in an interview with a Swiss newspaper on November 14, 2010:

> One must free oneself from the illusion that international climate policy is environmental policy. [What we're doing] has almost nothing to do with the climate. We must state clearly that we use climate policy to redistribute de facto the world's wealth.[21]

How come we have not heard this revealing statement proclaimed in our news media? This is not an opponent of climate change making this statement, but an advocate of it. If you are having trouble getting your head around this, try another one of his admissions:

> Climate policy has almost nothing to do anymore with protecting the environment. The next world climate summit in Cancun is actually an economy summit during which distribution of the world's resources will be negotiated.[22]

The high-ranking UN official admits that climate change has no real connection to the environment, but is just a cover for advancing the communistic tenet of redistribution of wealth. I think it is time we introduce Mr. Edenhofer's statements to America's college students. Climate change is not about saving the planet. It is about ending capitalism and ruling the planet. What is an absolute tragedy is the fact liberal Democrats support it 100 percent. The following words by John Eidson should be a wakeup call to every American citizen:

> No intelligent person can fail to recognize that the modern Democratic Party is using "climate change" as a ruse to fundamentally transform the United States of America into a socialist-cum-communist nation. But because the human ego is loath to admit when it's been duped, many patriotic liberals will continue allowing themselves to be led like sheep into the closing noose of the hammer and sickle. By the time they realize what happened, it will be too late.[23]

It is unsettling to realize the Democratic Party is an ally with the forces that would end our free market system and replace it with some socialistic brand that is more closely aligned with communism than not. They are trying to dupe us with climate change to have us surrender the best economic system the world has ever seen and take us back to oppression that rivals the old feudal system. How can that be progressive? The Democratic Party has chosen to be an anti-American movement with its advocating of climate change.

Another major reason for doubting climate change is the fraud executed by those in its ranks. *Investor's Business Daily* released an editorial on March 3, 2018, entitled, "The Stunning Statistical Fraud Behind The Global Warming Scare." It cites evidence of The National Oceanic and Atmospheric Administration fraudulently changing adjustments to data that favored global warming.[24] The following quote from the article reveals the malpractice of the agency:

> But the actual *measured* temperature record shows something different: There have been hot years and hot decades since the turn of the last century, and colder years and colder decades. But the overall measured temperature shows no clear trend over the last century, at least not one that suggests runaway warming.
>
> That is, until the NOAA's statisticians "adjust" the data. Using complex statistical models, they change the data to reflect not reality, but their underlying theories of global warming. That's clear from a simple fact of statistics: Data generate random errors, which cancel out over time. So by averaging data, the errors mostly disappear.[25]

The NOAA tampers with the data to gain a desired result that favors climate change. Recently NOAA added 2.5 degrees of fake warming to boost the global warming hoax.[26] Dr. Nils-Alex Mörner, the retired head of the paleogeophysics and geodynamics at Stockholm University who has measured sea levels for over fifty years, believes the UN's claims of sea levels rising because of CO_2 emissions by humans is totally misleading. He actually believes sea levels are declining instead of rising. He believes from his measurements and research that CO_2 has a minute effect on sea levels at best.[27] The following paragraph from the article coveys Dr. Mörner's conclusion:

> Mörner's conclusion is that solar activity and its effects on the globe have been the "dominant factor" in what happens to both the climate and the seas. Meanwhile, the UN claims the current changes in climate and sea level are attributable to human emissions of carbon dioxide (CO_2). Man's emissions

of this essential gas, required by plants and exhaled by people, makes up a fraction of 1 percent of all so-called greenhouse gases present naturally in the atmosphere. "Absolutely not," Mörner said about the CO_2 argument, noting there was "something basically sick" in the blame-CO_2 hypothesis. "CO_2, if it has any effect, it is minute—it does not matter. What has a big effect is the sun."[28]

Global warming is not settled science just because liberals want it to be. The fact is there is no such thing as settled science because there always looms a new discovery or experiment that brings new knowledge to the forefront.

The Greed Blame Game

Leftists worldwide, including those in the United States who have a comfortable home in the Democratic Party, have sought to put the blame for poverty on capitalism. Capitalism, for them, has just made too many rich people. For someone on the Left, a rich person had to get that way by exploiting someone else. This thinking is detestable. Rich people do not benefit from poor people. A rich person can only increase wealth when people buy the product or service he or she is selling, and that is not poor people. Liberal politicians love to take aim at the wealthy and vow punitive action on them in the name of the underprivileged. This tactic may gain some votes as the class-envy card is played, but it is totally bogus and unmerited.

It is socialism and communism that generate poverty in the masses, while capitalism has distinguished itself as the economic system that has raised more people out of poverty than any other. The following facts clearly show how beneficial capitalism is in relieving poverty:

1. The number of people living in extreme poverty worldwide declined by 80 percent from 1970 to 2006. People living on a dollar a day or less dramatically fell from 26.8 percent of the global population in 1970 to 5.4 percent in 2006—an 80 percent decline. It is a truly remarkable achievement that doesn't receive a lot of media coverage because it highlights the success of capitalism.

2. Poverty worldwide included 94 percent of the world's population in 1820. In 2011, it was only 17 percent. What is even more incredible is that the global poverty rate was 53 percent in 1981, causing the decline from 53 percent to 17 percent to be "the most rapid reduction in poverty in world history."

3. Globally, those in the lower- and middle-income brackets saw increases in pay of 40 percent from 1988 to 2008.

4. The world is 120 times better off today than in 1800 as a result of capitalism. Steven Horwitz of the Foundation for Economic Education (FEE), citing author Deidre McCloskey, noted that the 120 times figure comes from multiplying "the gains in consumption to the average human by the gain in life expectancy worldwide by 7 (for 7 billion as compared to 1 billion people)."

5. Mortality rates for children under the age of five declined by 49 percent from 1990 to 2013. This is according to World Health Organization (WHO) data, a decline termed "faster than ever."

Capitalism results in lower child mortality rates by promoting better access to medicine and higher standards of living.[29]

The critics of capitalism like to cite greed as its most abhorrent characteristic. Realistically, one does know greed has been a factor for some people and some companies who have engaged in business. Their greed has led them to pursue unethical and, in some cases, illegal tactics. We are a nation of laws so such practices can be curtailed. Just what is greed? Greed is defined as "a selfish and excessive desire for more of something (such as money) than is needed" (Merriam-Webster Dictionary).

The key word in this definition is "selfish." Much of the success of capitalism relates to people solving problems. We have all heard that "necessity is the mother of invention." A need exists and someone or some company finds a way to meet the need and gains a profit in the process. Those who have the need satisfied are benefited. When Sam Walton launched his first discount store, his motivation was not greed. He simply saw a retail niche whereby he could offer lower prices that would attract price-conscious consumers, and then he expanded the concept across the nation. As has been pointed out earlier, Walmart has operated a strong social responsibility program that has provided aid following many natural disasters. Where's the greed there?

The federal government levies an inheritance tax also known as a "death tax." When millionaires die, they can have their estate taxed up to 40 percent. Someone can start a company, work hard for its success, and legally and fairly reap enough profit to become a millionaire or even a billionaire. When this person dies, the federal government and some state governments write themselves into the will as if they are legitimate heirs. The money the person leaves behind is money that is rightfully theirs after they have paid taxes. The government is charging a fee for this person dying. How absurd! This was not the original intent of the Founding Fathers. Elizabeth Warren launched her campaign for president for 2020 with the idea of a wealth tax. She does not even want to wait for death. She wants to go take the money right now. She wants to legalize theft. Where's the real greed? Is it with Sam Walton or is it with the liberal Democrats? The answer is obvious. More greed can be found in liberal politicians than in the nation's capitalists.

Why is capitalism targeted by the Left? Capitalism provides people with the opportunity to pursue careers and create items that can lead to them accumulating wealth where they can maintain a comfortable lifestyle without any assistance from government. Government is to remain a fair and impartial referee in economic affairs. The liberal Left does not like this scenario. It wants to control the government and have it be referee and major player. It will then be allowed to control the economy, and, in essence, the lives of the people.

The next portion of this book will focus on the Constitution, which begins with the words "We the People." Liberals despise the Constitution because its purpose is to restrain the reach of government to preserve the liberty of the people. Liberals are more concerned about power for the party than benefit for the people. It is difficult to control people, who sustain their existence through their own work, which capitalism allows and encourages. If more and more people are to become dependent on big government, then capitalism needs to be eroded, if not eliminated. The Democratic Party is dedicated to this end. If capitalism is lost, liberty will not be far behind.

7

We the People

★

The Constitution of the United States begins with the words "We the People." These three words proclaimed that the United States of America would be a different country. It would be founded for the benefit of its people and not for those who would govern it. This was revolutionary at the time because most nations were ruled by a monarchy. The Constitution of the United States is the oldest active constitution in the world and one of the shortest in volume. It has been heralded as the greatest document for the protection of liberty for the citizens of a nation.

The pathway for its existence was not an easy road, but good things seldom come easily. On the Fourth of July every year, we participate in the celebration of the birthday of the United States. We mark the anniversary of the signing of the Declaration of Independence when our Founding Fathers proclaimed we were a free nation. Declaring itself a nation free from the rule of Great Britain and establishing the same were two different things. The United States had to win a war where the odds were strongly stacked against them. If that war was lost, the Fourth of July would have held no significance for the colonists in the

New World. But the war was won, and the task of forming an effective government was set before the Continental Congress.

While the Declaration was being drafted, another committee was charged with creating a form of government. In 1781 the Articles of Confederation became operational. This document was regarded to have many flaws, and the founders sought to correct them. They met in May of 1787 in Philadelphia to revise the Articles. One of the shortcomings of the original form of government provided by this document was that no executive leader was established. Congress was in charge of governing and courts were created when the need arose. There were no regulations regarding a national currency. States printed their own money, making intrastate commerce a nightmare. One state had the power to veto any proposed policy or law for the union. The Articles were very ineffective for establishing a unified nation that would create a strong national defense and manage domestic and foreign trade. It did not take the delegates long to realize that it made more sense to build a new house than remodel the old one. The goal was to draft a constitution that would outline the operation of a new government and then have the states ratify it.

A New National Government

The challenge in forming a new government through a constitution was that it had to be firm and efficient, that is to say, powerful enough and functional enough to execute the responsibilities given to it. This new government had to be strong enough to maintain national unity while safeguarding the rights and liberties of the people. The Constitution would set forth the form and operational procedure for governing. At the same time, it would set restrictions on the national government to protect the rights of the people and assure the individual states their authority to govern their own states with the powers not placed in the federal government. The Constitution was a restraining document on the federal government so a national government would be unable to muster enough power to overshadow the individual states without encroaching on the rights and liberties of the people.

The three basic functions that the national government was to be responsible for through the Constitution were national defense, foreign and intrastate trade, and domestic tranquility. The individual states could not establish strong armies and navies. They would be weak in facing foreign threats. If each state printed its own currency, trade among the states would be a hassle. If uprisings took place, individual states would likely be unprepared to deal with it. The philosophy of the founders was to frame a government that allowed the national government to have the power to take charge in these three basic areas, but allow the states to have much power to govern within their borders. This is all very clear in the words of James Madison in *Federalist Paper Number 45*:

> The powers delegated by the proposed Constitution to the federal government are few and defined. Those which are to remain in the State governments are numerous and indefinite. The former will be exercised principally on external objects, as war, peace, negotiation and foreign commerce. . . . The powers reserved to the several States will extend to all the objects normally concerning the lives, liberties, and properties of the People, as well as the internal order, improvement and prosperity of the states themselves.[1]

It is evident in the words of Madison that the new central government created by the Constitution was to be small government. That was the founders' original intent and it is opposite to the position of the liberal Left that controls today's Democratic Party. The founders only wanted enough federal government to create a union to deal with basic items, allowing the states to cover the rest. One could say that the founders thought "big government" was unconstitutional, from what Madison wrote. Another paragraph in *Federalist Paper Number 45* shows how Madison and the founders saw the limited role of federal government:

> The operations of the federal government will be at their most extensive and important in times of war and danger, while those of the state governments will be the most important in times of peace and security. Since periods of war and danger will probably occur much less than times of peace and security, the state governments will enjoy yet another advantage over the federal government. In fact, the more the federal government's powers are adequate for the national defense, the less frequently we'll be in periods of danger that require the federal government to use its maximum amount of power.[2]

Before we comment on these words, we need to say something about the *Federalist Papers*. After the Constitution was written and signed, it had to go before the states for adoption, or ratification. *The Federalist Papers*, which were written by Alexander Hamilton, James Madison, and John Jay, were the means of marketing to those who would vote on ratification why they should favor the new Constitution. The words of Madison, which we have just looked at, clearly reveal that the founders felt that the federal government was to have a limited role, though a very important and vital one. Madison was conveying that if the federal government is successful in doing its responsibility, it will be unnoticeable in favor of the states. It is obvious that the founders did not want a strong central government that was constantly poking its nose into the everyday business of the citizens and the states. If only such were true today!

The disdain for big government goes back to the Revolution and is noted in the Declaration of Independence. This document listed the grievances the colonies had against royal rule from England. One such complaint reads, "He has erected a multitude of New Offices to harass our people, and eat out their substance."

This criticism would be applicable today when examining Washington. To put it simply, the founders were no fans of federal bureaucracy and especially those that just kept growing and growing. Small government on the national level was the original intent of the founders and it was reflected in the Constitution. They were hopeful that this document would preserve this intent. Today, we live in a time when political forces on the Left oppose this intent of our founders, determined to undermine their work and their aspirations for our nation. To these forces, the Constitution is not a document to be revered but a target to distort, change, or destroy.

A Founding Document and the Framers

The Constitution was the founding document that established our nationhood and became the foundation for our success that followed. An argument could be made that the real birthday of our nation was September 17, 1787, when the Constitution was signed. But September

17 comes and goes every year and little attention is given to Constitution Day. New Hampshire became the ninth state to ratify the document in June 21, 1788, making it the law of the land. It could be argued that either of these two dates might be best as the nation's birthday.

The Constitution is the founding document that is critical to the life of our nation. It is our by-laws. It is the vanguard of our liberties. Vice President Pence, in a speech in Philadelphia on February 4, 2017, said of the Constitution that it was "the greatest bulwark against tyranny in history." He went on to say that it is the "best chapter of liberty the world has seen."[3] As fantastic as it is, there are those at work who would weaken it or eliminate it altogether. These people are not some foreign enemy, but some of our own citizens.

In the summer of 1787, representatives met in Philadelphia for what is now known as the Constitutional Convention. The ineffectiveness and the shortcomings of the Articles of Confederation were duly noted and corrective action took place. The framework of a new constitution began in May of 1787.

The creators of the Constitution, commonly known as the framers, did not put their necks at risk as the signers of the Declaration of Independence had. However, those who represented their state for those one hundred days, from May to September 1787, performed a vital service to keep our nation from being at risk. Those who attended the Constitutional Convention were not a reset of those who gave us the Declaration of Independence. Far from it, as only six who signed the Declaration attended the Constitutional Convention. Their names were George Clymer, Benjamin Franklin, Robert Morris, George Read, Roger Sherman, and James Wilson.

Fifty-five delegates attended the convention and only thirty-nine stayed and signed the finished document. Attendance was spotty at best. Rhode Island was the only state not to participate. It is noteworthy that some significant founders were not in attendance. John Adams was serving as minister to England, and Thomas Jefferson was doing the same in France. Samuel Adams and John Hancock were not present. Patrick Henry was elected as a delegate from Virginia, but declined to attend. He held misgivings as to what might be done at the gathering and did stand in opposition to the Constitution. James Madison provided insights about many who were present in his notes written throughout the time of the convention. Benjamin Franklin was the oldest delegate at age eighty-one; and the youngest was New Jersey's Jonathan Dayton, who was twenty-six.

In his book *The Framing of the Constitution of the United States,* Max Farrand provides insight into the delegates. George Washington did not sign the Declaration of Independence. He was a little busy putting an army together. His victory in the war gave him much popularity. He was elected to serve as the president and presiding officer at the convention. He was fifty-five years of age. He was reluctant to even be a delegate but was convinced by Virginia colleagues to accept since his presence was thought to be essential to the success of the meetings.

James Madison, who was also from Virginia, was the opposite of Washington. He was short and slender and must have presented quite the contrast to the six-foot-four Washington. These men were the only two who ascended to the presidency from among the convention delegates. Madison was known as a scholar and an effective speaker. His influence at the convention was powerful, and the final document held his intellectual imprint to the extent that he became known as the Father of the Constitution. He also took detailed notes about the proceedings and the debates that took place. Without this contribution, we would have far less knowledge about the convention. Historians are forever in his debt. He later distinguished himself as one of the writers of the *Federalist Papers*.

Another Virginian of note was sixty-two-year-old George Mason, who was the author of the Virginia Bill of Rights, which helped to influence the Bill of Rights that would be put into the Constitution later.

Gouverneur Morris, of Franklin's Pennsylvania, had a brilliant mind and was noted for his literary skills. His appearance was marred by a crippled arm and a wooden leg, but neither dampened his lively personality or dulled his wit. He is credited in history as the one who composed the wording of the document. The final form was inscribed by the skillful calligrapher Jacob Shallus of Pennsylvania.

A man of major influence at the convention, but even more so afterwards, was New York's Alexander Hamilton. He would be the catalyst behind the *Federalist Papers*. He favored a national government even stronger than the one created by the Constitution. He was determined to convince his state of New York to ratify the Constitution. New York was a large state and if it failed to ratify, then others might do the same.[4]

John Jay was not a delegate to the convention, but he merits examination in connection with the Constitution because he was the third author of the *Federalist Papers*. He also gained the respect of George Washington, who appointed him the first chief justice of the Supreme Court. As a New Yorker, he shared Hamilton's goal of convincing their state to ratify the Constitution. He would go on to become governor of the state of New York.

The words of the founders themselves give great insight into their core values. They provide a view into the context of the Constitution and invaluable clues as to the framers' original intent. James Madison's famous statement gives the reason that a constitution was necessary:

> If men were angels, no government would be necessary. If angels were to govern men, neither external nor internal controls on government would be necessary. In forming a government which is to be administered by men over men, the great difficulty lies in this: you must first enable government to control the governed; and in the next place oblige it to control itself."[5]

The wise Madison revealed his understanding of human nature and the imperfection related to it. We are no angels and neither are those who govern us. He supported government having the power or authority to exercise its task, but admonished that it must "control itself." Our nation is over 23 trillion dollars in debt. I wonder how Madison would feel about how well today's government is controlling itself. The intent of small government is clearly present in Madison's words.

George Washington, in his first draft of his inaugural address, echoed Madison's caution related to human nature and its potential for abuse of power:

> The blessed Religion revealed in the word of God will remain an eternal and awful monument to prove that the best Institution may be abused by human depravity; and that they may even, in some instances be made subservient to the vilest purposes.

Should, hereafter, those incited by the lust of power and prompted by the Supineness or venality of their Constituents, overleap the known barriers of this Constitution and violate the unalienable rights of humanity: it will only serve to shew, that no compact among men (however provident in its construction and sacred in its ratification) can be pronounced everlasting and inviolable, and if I may so express myself, that no Wall of words, that no mound of parchm[en]t can be so formed as to stand against the sweeping torrent of boundless ambition on the one side, aided by the sapping current of corrupted morals on the other.[6]

Washington believed anyone void of character and tainted by the lust for power would not let a document like the Constitution stand in his or her way. His words were a warning that corruption was possible and likely. His words "overleap the known barriers of this Constitution" are evidence that the Constitution was to be a constraint on government as a protection of the people's rights. If Washington were alive today and saw how liberals operated in the city that bears his name, he would be astounded just how prophetic his words were. The founders knew government was a necessity, but they were suspicious of it becoming so big and so powerful that it would jeopardize liberty. They took painful strides to form a government that would lessen the chance of corruption, but they knew it could not be totally eliminated. If corruption did arise, it would be the responsibility of the people to rectify it through the avenue set forth in the Constitution. Hamilton's words are applicable:

If the federal government should overpass the just bounds of its authority and make a tyrannical use of its powers, the people, whose creature it is, must appeal to the standard they have formed, and take such measures to redress the injury done to the Constitution as the exigency may suggest and prudence justify.[7]

Hamilton was a strong supporter of a federal government, but even he knew that there had to be limitations to its authority. He was also willing to link the success of the convention to help from God, stating, "For my own part, I sincerely esteem it [the Constitution] a system which without the finger of God, never could have been suggested and agreed upon by such a diversity of interests."[8]

Today, it is not possible to suggest a spiritual factor was in play at the convention, but Hamilton's words prove otherwise. John Adams did not participate in the convention but he undoubtedly approved of the results, and he also recognized the spiritual factor when he wrote, "Our Constitution was made only for a moral and religious people. It is wholly inadequate to the government of any other."[9] Adam's statement perhaps gives us some insight why we are having problems in achieving national unity today. Our nation was designed to work efficiently when we are religious and morally sound. John Jay, like Adams, was not at the convention, but his role in the *Federalist Papers* was very significant, and he too noted God's favor on the nation as he campaigned for the adoption of the Constitution in these essays. In *Federalist Paper Number 2*, he wrote:

This country and this people seem to have been made for each other, and it appears as if it was the design of Providence, that an inheritance so proper and convenient for a band of brethren, united to each other by the strongest ties, should never be split into a number of unsocial, jealous, and alien sovereignties.[10]

Jay believed that this nation was designed by God for the people who lived in it. He saw the people's unity in faith to be a reason to be united as a nation.

High Stakes and the Debate

Most Americans today likely have no idea how precarious the situation was for our young nation during the summer of 1787. The thirteen colonies had become states. They had united together to declare independence and fought a war to win it. But there was no guarantee that all thirteen would remain one nation or if states of a particular region would want to form their own nation. Northern states and southern states differed on the issue of slavery. The oppression of a tyrannical government was fresh in the mind of the delegates. They did not wish to create a government that would be a home-grown version of the one they had suffered under and defeated for their freedom. The preservation of state rights was a high priority of many delegates, but at the same time it was obvious that individual states would be at a major disadvantage when it came to military and foreign commerce affairs.

The stakes were high when the convention began. The future of America hung in the balance. If the delegates got it wrong, then what was won at such a great cost in war could be lost forever. The framers were well aware of the seriousness of the situation. Madison and Hamilton both voiced that they "were now to decide forever the fate of the Republican Government."[11] Gouverneur Morris said, "The whole human race will be affected by the proceedings of this Convention."[12]

There were more differences to reconcile besides the issue of slavery.

176

There was the contention between large states and small states. Large states did not like the one-state veto in the Articles of Confederation. They did not feel a small state should have such power. States of lesser population did not want to be viewed as insignificant. Some delegates were strong federalists and others were solid for state rights (Anti-Federalists). The delegates had all seen corruption at work firsthand in England's heavy-handed rule. They wanted to limit the possibility of such happening in the new government they were about to design. Some would have enthusiastically made George Washington king, which would establish a noble class. The challenge was great, but in the end, so were the results.

The two plans that received the most consideration were the Virginia Plan and the New Jersey Plan. This latter plan favored an executive leadership composed of three people. It would be presidency by committee. It would have state governors appointed by a centralized committee. It also gave more power to a centralized federal government where Congress could levy taxes on states if necessary. It would have power to be punitive to delinquent states.[13]

The Virginia Plan was more states-rights friendly and won the day. This plan made provision for the three branches of government: legislative, executive, and judicial. The legislature was to be composed of two houses, the House of Representatives, to be elected every two years by the people, and the Senate, to which each state legislature would elect two senators. It was not until 1913 that senators were to be elected directly by the people, which became law through the Seventeenth Amendment. Representatives were elected from districts in their states, and the numbers of districts were set by a ten-year census. One of the times when an amendment has had disastrous consequences was the passage of the Seventeenth Amendment, as it made neither house of Congress accountable to or concerned with adherence to the Tenth Amendment!

The delegates sought a system of government that had checks and balances so no branch of government could become all-powerful. The two houses in the legislature checked one another since a bill had to pass both houses to become law. The president could check the legislature by vetoing a passed bill. The House and Senate could override the president's veto with a two-thirds vote. The judicial branch could review laws and rule for their constitutionality. The president could have the power to appoint judges with approval of the Senate. Officials, including the president and judges, could be removed by an impeachment process. (Note: Impeachment is not removal from office. It is a part of a process for removal from office. The House can impeach, which is a charge of wrongdoing thought to be serious enough for removal. The Senate tries the case, functioning as jury. A two-thirds vote of senators present is needed for conviction and subsequent removal. The checks and balances make for the wheels of government to move slowly. This is by design so no wave of illogical emotion could carry the day.)

The Great Compromise was the two-house legislature. It satisfied the states with large populations and the small ones with fewer inhabitants. In the House of Representatives, each state would have one representative for every forty thousand inhabitants. This included slaves counting as three-fifths of a person. Of course, this gave larger states more representatives in the House and thus more voting power. The Senate was composed of two senators for each state, giving each state equal voting power in this chamber.

The three-fifths slave valuation was hotly debated. Gouverneur Morris was an ardent critic of slavery. He felt that slaves should be considered equal to white citizens for census purposes. If slaves were property, then some from the New England states wondered if they could count their cattle.[14] Many today see this three-fifths designation as appalling and an act of bigotry. But the actual reasoning was aimed at limiting slavery. Northern delegates from free states did not want southern states to use slaves, who could not vote, to boost their census population, resulting in more representatives giving slave states more voting power in the House. Slavery may have expanded to all new states, and the issue may have been harder to resolve even though it is hard to imagine a worse event than the Civil War. The Free State delegates would have rather had the slaves not count at all so they could not be exploited by the southern states to increase their House of Representative seats for more political power.

Historians have pointed out the real reason the slavery issue was not directly dealt with by those founders who opposed it. If they had pushed the issue in 1776, it would have killed any chance for the Revolution to succeed. If it was pressed at the Constitutional Convention in 1787, the nation would not have been established.[15] Great Britain was a well-established nation and arguably the strongest in the world. It resolved its slavery issue with a Wilberforce, where we had to do so by the force of war.

The delegates at the convention debated and labored through the summer of 1787 and concluded their work on September 17, 1787. The struggle was not over. The document had to be ratified by the states, which meant that the debate would leave Philadelphia and spill over into the legislative halls of each of the thirteen states. The ratification of the Constitution was not guaranteed. The Federalists and Anti-Federalists would continue to clash during the ratification process. Noted names such as Patrick Henry and Samuel Adams were on the side opposing ratification.

The delegates, with this new constitution, created a federal government endowed with powers that would affect the states. The completed document endowed the national government with "enumerated powers," which included the authority to tax internally and externally (via excises and tariffs), regulate foreign and interstate commerce, enforce contracts and property rights, form armies in time of peace and war, make treaties, and make all laws "necessary and proper" to carry out these powers. This prevented the states from levy tariff and customs duties, coin and print money, or impairs contracts (via debtors' laws). These changes had far-reaching results.

Ratification Struggle

The Anti-Federalists may have felt they lost out at the Constitutional Convention, but they could redeem their loss if they could influence enough states to not ratify the document. Nine states were needed to ratify the Constitution for it to become law. The Federalists were not going to sit by passively and just hope that ratification would happen. They embarked on what we today would call a marketing campaign. Hamilton, Madison, and Jay all favored the Constitution being ratified. They joined forces to write what is known as *The Federalist Papers*, which proclaimed the virtues of the drafted Constitution. These eighty-five essays were published in newspapers under the name of Publius. *The Federalist Papers* made the case that a form of centralized government was necessary and that the one outlined in the drafted Constitution was well suited to be embraced. *The Federalist Papers,* along with the Constitution, have been an influence for individual rights around the world, since they have been translated into more than twelve languages, including Chinese.

Beck and Charles reveal the importance of *The Federalist Papers* in their book, *The Original Argument:*

> Ultimately, the Federalist Papers were about transparency. Unlike now, when several-thousand-page bills are routinely passed without citizens (and sometimes even legislators) knowing what's in them, our Founders wanted the public to know exactly what they would be getting. The Papers gave citizens a chance to hear the best arguments in support of the Constitution and understand how the new government would actually function. They outlined what a balanced government would look like and explained why certain powers belonged to the federal government while others should remain with the states. Best of all, the Papers were written in a clear voice that lacked pretense and was easy for most Americans (well, at least most eighteenth-century Americans) to understand.[16]

It is a shame that most Americans today are unaware of these papers and their value to understanding the Constitution. Today, if you were to ask college students who are not history majors, "What were *The Federalists Papers?*" I don't think 10 percent would have any idea.

New Hampshire ratified the Constitution on June 21, 1788, and, as the ninth state to do so, made it the law of the land. The two large states of Virginia and New York also ratified the document soon after, which enhanced its credibility. The efforts of the Anti-Federalists were not without significance. It was through their efforts that a Bill of Rights was added to the first ten amendments, which were ratified and became effective on December 15, 1791.

The words of the founders provide insight into just how extraordinary this founding document is to our nation. George Washington, who presided as the president of the convention and became the nation's first president, said, "The Constitution is the guide which I never will abandon."[17] The Constitution does not make a direct reference to God as does the Declaration of Independence, but the words of James Madison reveal that divine influence was considered as a factor: "It is impossible for the man of pious reflection not to perceive in it [the Constitution] a finger of that Almighty hand which has been so frequently and signally extended to our relief in the critical stages of the revolution."[18] Madison was aware that God's involvement was just as active in the framing of the Constitution as it was in the outcome of the Revolutionary War.

Let's revisit the words of John Adams: "Our Constitution was made only for a moral and religious people. It is wholly inadequate to the government of any other."[19] His comments indicate how strongly God's influence was regarded back in his day. They stand in stark contrast to our society today.

Thomas Jefferson was serving diplomatic duty when the convention was in session, but his words show his support for it:

> The example of changing a constitution by assembling the wise men of the state, instead of assembling armies, will be worth as

much to the world as the former examples we had given them. The constitution, too, which was the result of our deliberation, is unquestionably the wisest ever presented to men.[20]

When the convention was over, the oldest delegate, Benjamin Franklin, was asked by a woman what kind of government had been given the nation. Franklin replied, "A Republic, madam, if you can keep it."[21] Franklin's conditional clause, "if you can keep it," has never been more relevant and pertinent in America's existence than it is now. As we will focus on in a later chapter, we have people in our nation involved in the political process who would like to see the United States not remain a republic. They regard the Constitution as an enemy. The Constitution is bedrock law for our nation, designed to give government a workable structure that still preserves the liberty of the people by restraining the reach of a centralized government.

8

Preserving Liberty

★

Many of the Federalists, including Hamilton, felt there was no need for a bill of rights to be added to the Constitution. The Anti-Federalists prevailed. Their efforts did indeed enhance the Constitution and help to protect the liberties of the people. After the Constitution was ratified, it was not the end of the political dynamic. Many wanted the assurance that basic liberties would be spelled out and therefore protected. Some states even wanted to call another convention to redo the Constitution to make sure that cherished liberties would be included. The Federalists did not want this because they feared that much of what took many days to create could be undone. Many of them thought that such a convention could put the newly formed government in peril. This led many Federalists to compromise with the Anti-Federalists to allow for a number of amendments to be included and stand as a bill of rights.

James Madison, who was so instrumental in the debate and in drafting the Constitution, and who made significant contributions to *The Federalist Papers* to encourage ratification, played a vital role in the inclusion of the Bill of Rights. He almost did not gain a seat in the new Congress, which would consider the issue while he was unable to win a senate seat. He did finally prevail in his district for a seat in the House of Representatives. He pushed for the Bill of Rights amendments because of his promise to his Virginia constituency, who had voiced their support for such action.[1]

Today, the Constitution and the Bill of Rights are regarded as one entity that works to protect the liberties of the people while restraining the power of a centralized government.[2] We are so fortunate that the Bill of Rights was added, because it gives clarity to what rights were regarded as foundational to our freedom. If the founders could have looked into the future and seen what we are dealing with today, there could easily have been three more amendments: (1) the right for a conceived fetus to be born, protected from abortion; (2) the right for the sanctity of marriage between one man and one woman to be protected; and (3) the right for people to be protected from the adversity of illegal immigration into the nation. The preamble of the Constitution states part of the purpose for establishing the union was to "insure domestic Tranquility, provide for the common defense . . ."

The Anti-Federalists were right to press for a bill of rights to be included in the Constitution, and they provided future citizens a great service. Rights clearly stated are far more difficult to remove by sinister political forces. If these rights were just assumed to exist, they could easily be eroded away. Can you imagine what would take place today if the Second Amendment did not exist and clearly state bearing arms is a right?

The framers did not make amending the Constitution an easy endeavor. This was on purpose so emotional whims could not rule the day. Today, some states can have state constitutions amended by the vote of the people. Changes are made not by thoughtful wisdom, but by which side can afford the slickest marketing campaign. Article V of the Constitution explains the procedure for amending the Constitution. Basically, it requires both houses of Congress to propose an amendment by two-thirds vote, which is then ratified by three-fourths of the state legislatures.

The Bill of Rights: Amendments 1–5

In this chapter, we will consider the amendments to the Constitution and briefly look at each one's purpose. We start with the first ten amendments, also known as the Bill of Rights.

> Congress shall make no law respecting an establishment of religion, or prohibiting the free exercise thereof; or abridging the freedom of speech or of the press; or the right of the people to peaceably assemble, and to petition the Government for a redress of grievances.
>
> First Amendment to the US Constitution

In chapter 3 we looked at the religious aspects of this amendment. It was pointed out that Congress, i.e., the federal government, was restricted from establishing a religion and from prohibiting one from exercising his or her religion. In Supreme Court rulings, it has been the federal government that has violated this amendment. In the case of *Reed v. Van Hoven*, 1965, the focus was on an Alabama boy who prayed over his lunch at school. It was ruled that he was not to say the prayer out loud. In no way was this boy establishing a religion. He was exercising his religion. The amendment denies the federal government authority to effect this action. You will recall that some states had and continued to have state official churches that the federal government did not require to be discontinued after the new government was established. Evidence was provided that the founders regarded the establishment of a religion to mean recognizing one denomination as the official church for the nation like some European nations had.

James Madison is credited with the wording of this First Amendment, so it would be valuable to know his feelings on this issue. His beliefs are revealed in the following citation:

> Madison believed it was the duty of civil government to protect liberty, especially religious liberty, so that no one's freedom would be impaired. The government should not endorse one church over another so that "all men should enjoy the fullest toleration in the exercise of religion according to the dictates of conscience, unpunished and unrestrained by the magistrate, unless under the color of religion any man disturb the peace, the happiness, or safety of society . . ."[3]

Madison concurred with other founders that the establishment action was in reference to designating one denomination as the official national church, which would be favored with political power and revenue benefits. It was not intended to be used to oust the Christian faith from the public square or from involvement in civic affairs as it is today. The vital question to be asked here is, "When the federal government is restricted from an action by this amendment, why does it think it can use this amendment to deny the states, school districts, and citizens from allowing this action to take place?" Today, the federal government uses this amendment to prevent a liberty (religious) from being enjoyed, when the purpose of the Bill of Rights was to protect the people from having the federal government infringing on their rights.

Congress (federal government) is restricted from making laws resulting in "abridging the freedom of speech or of the press." The founders believed that the constitutional system depended on a self-governing people who would exercise control over government and what the Constitution provides. Freedom of speech and a free press were seen as necessary for this.[4] This part of the First Amendment appears so basic to a free people that it is taken for granted by most citizens, but it is not without its adversaries today. We will examine, in the next chapter, those forces that wish to advance policies or practices that would deny some this right. As technology creates more opportunities for the "press" to expound, more information is provided, often without the companion of truth.

A free press is not required to be a proclaimer of truth. Today, a consumer of information is best served by a healthy dose of skepticism. The founders hoped that a free press would serve the people by keeping government accountable. Presently, some press (media) seeks to protect and not make some participants in government accountable through biased reporting. With a right to a free press, this action is legal. It may not best serve the public, but it is not against the law. Today, we have the battle of the media where both liberals and conservatives each have their own media benefactors. How these media benefactors position and divest themselves will be dealt with later.

The First Amendment also states "the right of the people to peaceably assemble, and to petition the Government for a redress of grievances." This part of the amendment endorses the basic concept of government by the people. This right is denied by tyrannical governments. People coming together can make for change. Dr. Martin Luther King Jr., with his march on Washington on August 28, 1963, and his "I Have a Dream," speech is an example of this. The "redress of grievance" can take place in petition. Such can be done through tedious signed paper copies connected to a complaint or via the technology of the day, by online procedures. One could also claim that grievances can be addressed through public opinion polls. Reliable polls can bring to the attention of government leaders the sentiment of the people, which can motivate these leaders to take action in harmony with the will of the people.

The Second Amendment receives a great deal of attention today. It states:

> A well regulated Militia, being necessary to the security of a free State, the right of the people to keep and bear Arms, shall not be infringed.

The possession of arms allowed the colonists to effectively rebel against England. The founders knew that a citizenry devoid of the right to bear arms would be vulnerable to an oppressive government should one come to power and want to expand that power.

> Shortly after the US Constitution was officially ratified, James Madison proposed the Second Amendment as a way to empower these state militias. While the Second Amendment did not answer the broader Anti-Federalist concern that the federal government had too much power, it did establish the principle (held by both Federalists and their opponents) that the government did not have the authority to disarm citizens.[5]

190

The words "regulated Militia" are key to the gun control/right to bear arms debate. A militia was seen as a vital means of defense for a community by the founders. There are those who say that a National Guard now covers this and the average Joe does not need to be packing heat. The other side of the argument believes that citizens who have arms can become a part of a defense force for community or personal property and self, when such a need should arise. Decisions by the Supreme Court have supported this position, and the prevailing belief by both Federalists and Anti-Federalists is that the government has no right to disarm its people. When this amendment is taken literally, there is no restriction on what type of arms a citizen can own.

The contentious discussion regarding the Second Amendment in our current times is more focused on political issues than on constitutional precepts. This amendment comes into the crosshairs of the liberals seemingly more than any other as they seek to transform the nation. Their purpose and tactics will be examined more closely in the next chapter. The right to bear arms as provided by the Second Amendment was seen by the founders as essential to people living in freedom in America. Thomas Jefferson said, "No free man shall ever be debarred the use of arms."[5] Jefferson does not tie his remarks to only use in a militia. It is interesting to remember Jefferson was the founder of the Democratic Party. Today, when Democrats have their county dinners, they are called the Jefferson-Jackson Dinner after these two famous presidents.

One of the catalysts of the Revolution, Samuel Adams, proclaimed, "The said Constitution [shall] be never construed to authorize Congress to infringe the just liberty of the press, or the rights of conscience; or to prevent the people of the United States, who are peaceable citizens, from keeping their own arms."[6] He knew firsthand how important having arms was when Redcoats aimed their rifles at the colonists.

Noah Webster, the man who published the first dictionary and who was a good friend of Alexander Hamilton, provided some insightful comments on this issue:

> Before a standing army can rule, the people must be disarmed; as they are in almost every kingdom in Europe. The supreme power in America cannot enforce unjust laws by the sword; because the whole body of the people are armed, and constitute a force superior to any band of regular troops that can be, on any pretence, raised in the United States. A military force, at the command of Congress, can execute no laws, but such as the people perceive to be just and constitutional; for they will possess the power.[7]

Webster was saying for people to be oppressed and controlled by government they have to be disarmed. An armed citizenry is insurance against government seeking to enforce unjust laws. In Webster's thinking, if people are to have the power, then they must be free to arm themselves.

The Third Amendment reads:

> No soldier shall, in time of peace be quartered in any house, without the consent of the Owner, nor in time of war, but in a manner to be prescribed by law.

This amendment emerges from adverse historical experience encountered by the founders. The British military would require colonists to room and board soldiers in their houses. This was true during the French and Indian War and was in practice up to the Revolutionary War. This action by the British was one of the complaints listed in the Declaration of Independence. The founders wanted to be sure no quartering of soldiers would take place under the new federal government.

This issue is not in play at all in our nation and it arose only once in our history. During a strike of New York State correction officers in 1979, the National Guard was called in and quartered in housing that was occupied by the correction guards who were evicted to make these accommodations available. The court case of *Engblom v. Carey* made it to the Court of Appeals level where the ruling was in favor of the defendants. The belief was that the guardsmen were soldiers and because of qualified immunity could not be sued if they were performing state-prescribed duty.[8] This is the only time the Third Amendment has been brought into question in our nation's history.

The Fourth Amendment is best known to Americans as the "probable cause amendment." It deals with one's privacy that requires law enforcement to obtain a search warrant to investigate the contents of one's house and other possessions. This amendment states:

> The right of the people to be secure in their persons, houses, papers, and effects, against unreasonable searches and seizures, shall not be violated, and no Warrants shall issue, but upon probable cause, supported by Oath of affirmation, and particularly describing the place to be searched, and the persons or things to be seized.

This right is a result of what the founders felt was an extreme reach of the British government that ruled the colonies. The basis for this amendment for a person's protection of privacy, residence, and possession is seen in the following statement:

> General warrants allowed the Crown's messengers to search without any cause to believe someone had committed an offense. In those cases the judges decided that such warrants violated English common law. In the colonies the Crown used the writs of assistance—like general warrants, but often unbounded by time restraints—to search for goods on which taxes had not been paid. James Otis challenged the writs in a Boston court; though he lost, some such as John Adams attribute this legal battle as the spark that led to the Revolution. Both controversies led to the famous notion that a person's home is their castle, not easily invaded by the government.[9]

The Fourth Amendment is thought by some to give criminals an advantage. On the surface, it may first appear to be this way, but policing and law enforcement have developed sophisticated procedures and technologies to offset this perceived advantage. It needs to be pointed out that modern times have created an environment far different from the one in which the amendment was first introduced. Though crime did exist in our nation's early years, it was not as prevalent as it is today. There were no elaborate police forces like we have today. Citizen watches, a few constables, and some sheriffs made up law enforcement in the early days of the nation.

The execution of the Fourth Amendment is far more complicated today than the founders ever could have imagined. Today, we have smart phones that contain records of calls and Internet searches. Computers contain files, emails, and search records that could be used as evidence. Phone lines can be wired tapped with the permission of warrants. So much of what we have now that can be used as evidence in a trial did not exist in 1791.

The probable cause concept does indeed benefit every individual in America in an overall fashion even though modern times make deciphering certain situations more difficult. Most of us have faced a search when we went to board a flight at the airport. Why does TSA get to make such searches without a warrant? A court ruling clearly explains why security at airports can search away:

> In 1973 the 9th Circuit Court rules on *U.S. v. Davis*, 482 F.2d 893, 908, there are key pieces of wording that give the TSA its power to search essentially any way they choose to. The key wording in this ruling includes "noting that airport screenings are considered to be administrative searches because they are conducted as part of a general regulatory scheme, where the essential administrative purpose is to prevent the carrying of weapons or explosives aboard aircraft."

> *U.S. v. Davis* goes on to state, "[An administrative search is allowed if] no more intrusive or intensive than necessary, in light of current technology, to detect weapons or explosives, confined in good faith to that purpose, and passengers may avoid the search by electing not to fly."[10]

It clearly points out you don't have to fly, but if you do fly, you are willingly submitting to a search by TSA. Since being searched is a requirement for boarding, and because it is a means for protecting other passengers, you are consenting to the search, which removes it from the coverage of the Fourth Amendment.

The Fifth Amendment is the favorite one of politicians and others who are subpoenaed to testify before Congress. It reads:

> No person shall be held to answer for a capital, or otherwise infamous crime, unless on a presentment or indictment of a grand jury, except in cases arising in the land or naval forces, or in the militia, when in actual service in time of war or public danger; nor shall any person be subject for the same offense to be twice put in jeopardy of life or limb; nor shall be compelled in any criminal case to be a witness against himself, nor be deprived of life, liberty, or property, without due process of law; nor shall private property be taken for public use, without just compensation.

It gives a person the right not to testify on the grounds that such testimony might incriminate him or her. This might appear to be an admission of guilt to most people. However, the burden of proof of guilt still rests on those doing the prosecuting or interrogating. This portion of the amendment is known as the "self-incrimination clause" whereby an accused is protected against himself or herself. In essence, it is saying a person cannot be forced to provide evidence against his own person.

The first part of the amendment deals with the use of a grand jury. When a person is charged with a crime, the evidence is presented before a grand jury, which decides if the accused should be indicted and stand trial. A grand jury is made up of ordinary citizens just as trial juries are for cases tried in court.

Another part of this amendment relates to "double jeopardy," which means a person cannot be tried for the same crime twice. This is why law enforcement goes to great lengths to make sure they have a strong case against an accused. One might be found innocent in criminal court, but could then face charges in a civil court in some incidents. These would be regarded as different charges and double jeopardy would not be violated.

The amendment also gives attention to "due process," which is provided to protect a person's right to not be treated unfairly in the legal process. Due process is described below:

> Due process, a course of legal proceedings according to rules and principles that have been established in a system of jurisprudence for the enforcement and protection of private rights. In each case, due process contemplates an exercise of the powers of government as the law permits and sanctions, under recognized safeguards for the protection of individual rights. Principally associated with one of the fundamental guarantees of the United States Constitution, due process derives from early English common law and constitutional history.[11]

Defense lawyers are very keen on due process. If it is violated, the case and charges against his or her client could be dismissed.

And the key to forever ending the scourge of abortion in our nation lies in the Fifth as well as the Fourteenth Amendments. The simple solution is recognizing that the unborn child is in fact a PERSON. Personhood would mean that no abortion could take place without "due process" for the one whose life is being ended arbitrarily. We should pray daily that Congress, the courts, and our culture will soon recognize what science already does—personhood begins at conception. We will discuss this critical issue of personhood later in our discussion of the *Roe v. Wade* abortion case from 1973.

The Bill of Rights: Amendments 6–10

The Sixth Amendment also relates to legal matters. It guarantees an accused person the "right to a speedy and public trial, by an impartial jury." The accused is to "be informed of the nature and cause of the accusation; to be confronted with the witnesses against him; to have compulsory process for obtaining witnesses in his favor, and to have the assistance of counsel for his defense." This amendment sets some of the basic rules for a court case. The founders took great care to make sure that anyone accused of a crime would get a fair review in court and an opportunity to prove his innocence. They had seen firsthand how the British Crown misused the justice system and they sought ways to prevent this.

The Seventh Amendment continues along these lines by giving an accused person the right to trial by a jury if the involved controversy is more than twenty dollars. The Eighth Amendment also has a legal focus as it prevents "excessive bail" and "excessive fines." It also prohibits "cruel and unusual punishments." This amendment has garnered attention regarding the punishment aspect. Some states have eliminated the death penalty from their justice system and cite this amendment as the reason.

After the Constitution and the Bill of Rights were ratified, those who committed capital offenses were sentenced to death, and the sentence was carried out much faster than such sentences are today. Hanging was a common form of capital punishment in the early days of the nation after the Constitution was operative. It seems strange that this form of execution was not regarded by the founders as cruel and unusual. It comes down to who has the power to decide what is cruel and unusual, and often states make these decisions without regard to history and precedence.

Utah executed a man by firing squad in 2010. Firing squad execution is on the books in Oklahoma. Some southern states are taking a look at it since there has been controversy with lethal drug executions that have been botched.[12]

The Ninth Amendment simply states:

> The enumeration in the Constitution, of certain rights, shall not be construed to deny or disparage others retained by the people.

What this amendment means is that the rights listed in the Constitution are not all-inclusive. The people may have other rights they enjoy that government cannot take away. You have the right to eat whatever diet you wish. You have the right to sport any hairstyle you want. You have the right to vacation in any state you wish. You get the idea, but don't think such things are beyond government targeting. New York City has banned sugary soft drinks that are over sixteen ounces.[13] It seems a bit ridiculous, when you could buy two sixteen-ounce drinks and consume one after the other. Logic, however, has not always been a welcome guest in politics.

The last amendment that composes the Bill of Rights is the Tenth Amendment. It contains few words but holds a major precept in our nation's concept of liberty. It states:

> The powers not delegated to the United States by the
> Constitution, nor prohibited by it to the States, are reserved to
> the States respectively, or to the people.

When we look at the Constitutional Convention and study the
debate, we see that there was great concern about how much power the
federal government would have, and to what degree it would infringe
on the power of the states. The Federalists and Anti-Federalists were set
on the two sides of this debate. *The Federalists Papers* were published to
convince the states and the people that the federal government would
have few powers and the states would have vast powers in comparison.
This amendment in essence was giving written assurance of this. The
Framers of the Constitution had the federal government holding few
powers, consisting mainly of national defense, foreign trade, treaties
with foreign nations, domestic tranquility issues, which were beyond
the scope of the states, and setting laws that enhanced trade among the
individual states, like printing one currency.

Today, the argument could be made the Tenth Amendment is the
most violated amendment in the Constitution. The culprit is the federal
government. Where in the Constitution does the federal government
get the right to run a retirement program, a health care system, a food
stamp program, an agricultural subsidy program, to tell states what
their schools can post on a bulletin board and a host of other items,
some of which border on the ridiculous, like forcing states to provide
public school education to illegal immigrants?

In 1887 Congress passed the Texas Seed Bill to help farmers in Texas
who were devastated by a drought. The amount was not very much,

only a little over $200,000 in today's money. Democrat President Grover Cleveland vetoed the bill and he said why:

> I can find no warrant for such an appropriation in the Constitution; and I do not believe that the power and duty of the General Government ought to be extended to the relief of individual suffering which is in no manner properly related to the public service or benefit. A prevalent tendency to disregard the limited mission of this power and duty should, I think, be steadily resisted, to the end that the lesson should be constantly enforced that, though the people support the Government, the Government should not support the people.[14]

It is unbelievable for us today to think that a Democratic president would take such an action. President Cleveland was in harmony with the Tenth Amendment, believing that there was no Constitutional authority to give a handout to one group of people. States might have the power to do this, but for Cleveland, it was beyond what the federal government was entitled to do based on the Constitution. He might find life difficult in today's Democratic Party, or for that matter in the Republican Party. Cleveland felt charitable contributions from fellow citizens should be the focus of an appeal to bring relief, and this was done. The result was people gave ten times the amount that Congress would have provided in the bill.[15] This proves that government cannot even do charity as well as the private sector of ordinary American citizens.

The words of Robert Allen Rutland in his book *The Birth of the Bill of Rights 1776–1791* give insight into what the Bill of Rights would do for the American people:

> However, they foresaw change, believing that in the Bill of Rights

201

great standards of personal freedom had been established. Their hope was that an enlightened and responsible citizenry could uphold the enduring values of the Bill of Rights regardless of the circumstnces.[16]

The question to be answered today is, "Are we that responsible citizenry dedicated to upholding these enduring values?" When I see people elected to high federal office who proudly proclaim they want to fundamentally transform our nation, I wonder just how responsible we are. I fear that far too many voters, who cast ballots, fall far short of the hope our founders had when they gave us the Bill of Rights. We must work to correct this.

The most important takeaway from the Bill of Rights? Read them all carefully. In every one of them, the power of GOVERNMENT is what is being limited. In not ONE of them is a citizen or his or her rights limited, but rather guaranteed. The Bill of Rights was written as a restraint on government in order to protect the rights of the individual. NEVER forget that!

Amendments 11 and 12

After the Bill of Rights, seventeen more amendments were made to the Constitution. Let's briefly look at them and note what impact they may have had. The Eleventh Amendment places a restriction on the jurisdiction of a federal court hearing and ruling on certain cases related to the states. This amendment was ratified in 1795 just a few years after the Bill of Rights. It was in keeping with the spirit promoted by the Framers that protected state rights in light of an existing federal government. The following paragraphs explain this amendment:

The text of the Eleventh Amendment limits the power of federal courts to hear lawsuits against state governments brought by the citizens of another state or the citizen of a foreign country. The Supreme Court has also interpreted the Eleventh Amendment to bar federal courts from hearing lawsuits instituted by citizens of the state being sued and lawsuits initiated by the governments of foreign countries. For example, the state of New York could invoke the Eleventh Amendment to protect itself from being sued in federal court by its own residents, residents of another state, residents of a foreign country, or the government of a foreign country.

The Eleventh Amendment is rooted in the concept of Federalism, under which the US Constitution carefully enumerates the powers of Congress to govern at the national level, while safeguarding the power of states to govern locally. By limiting power of federal courts to hear lawsuits brought against state governments, the Eleventh Amendment attempts to strike a balance between the sovereignty shared by the state and federal government.[17]

The Twelfth Amendment was created to fix a flaw in the election system related to the president and vice president. Article II of the Constitution was altered by this amendment. The Twelfth Amendment created two separate ballots for the office of president and the office of vice president. Originally, no one ran for vice president. That office was awarded to the person with the second highest votes for president. The election of 1800 necessitated a change. In this election, Thomas Jefferson got seventy-three electoral votes, as did Aaron Burr. This meant that the election of president went to the House of Representatives. Finally, Jefferson prevailed in this chamber. He became president and Burr vice president.[18]

This undoubtedly did not make for the best working relationship between the president and the vice president. Burr almost became president but will instead be known for killing Alexander Hamilton in a gun duel in July of 1804. The amendment was ratified that summer about four weeks before the duel and in time for that year's election.

Amendments for Full Freedom: 13, 14, 15

On April 9, 1865, Lee surrendered to Grant, ending the Civil War. It would be December of that year before the Thirteenth Amendment would be added to the Constitution. It is related to the slavery issue. It reads:

> Section 1. Neither slavery nor involuntary servitude, except as a punishment for crime whereof the party shall have been duly convicted, shall exist within the United States, or any place subject to their jurisdiction.

> Section 2. Congress shall have power to enforce this article by appropriate legislation.

This amendment outlawed slavery. By making it part of the Constitution, this guaranteed all rights given to a citizen now also belonged to those who were once slaves, and never would this atrocity be permitted in the nation ever again. An exception is made in the amendment for punishment for lawbreakers who have been convicted of a crime. As a boy, Steve took trips to visit relatives in Florida, and his father pointed out the chain gangs of prisoners in Georgia doing roadside cleanup. Community service, which is used today for some low offense sentencing, would be another example of the exemption.

The Fourteenth Amendment holds great significance historically and in the present day. This amendment came within three years of the previous one and also was connected to the slavery issue. It is one of the longest worded amendments in the Constitution, but its first section holds the main content, which provides its impact:

> All persons born or naturalized in the United States, and subject to the jurisdiction thereof, are citizens of the United States and of the state wherein they reside. No state shall make or enforce any law which shall abridge the privileges or immunities of citizens of the United States; nor shall any state deprive any person of life, liberty, or property, without due process of law; nor deny to any person within its jurisdiction the equal protection of the laws.

The Thirteenth Amendment freed the slaves and the Fourteenth Amendment made them official citizens, ending the three-fifths destination for population counting. This amendment secured civil rights for the Negros (as they were called back when the amendment was ratified). Some southern states did their best to make the full experience of civil rights very difficult, which had to be dealt with in future civil rights legislation. The key clause in the amendment is the "Due Process Clause," which prevents a state from depriving any person of life, liberty, or property without due process of law. This was originally related to professional contracts and transactions. However, it has become, over time, more closely connected to right-to-privacy cases. This right-to-privacy concept is what seven Supreme Court justices used to legalize abortion. The next chapter will deal with this perplexing, illogical ruling in more detail.[19]

The Fifteenth Amendment was ratified in 1870 and was the last one tied to the slavery issue with a focus on voting rights:

> Section 1. The right of citizens of the United States to vote shall not be denied or abridged by the United States or by any State on account of race, color, or previous condition of servitude.

No one could be denied the right to vote based on race. Southern states, during the period of reconstruction, would seek ways to suppress the votes of blacks, but this amendment made such actions illegal.

Amendments 16–22

It would be forty-three years before another amendment would become part of the Constitution. This amendment, the Sixteenth, hit most American families in the pocketbook. It is the amendment that allows the United States government to levy an income tax. The first tax was operational in 1913 and it consisted of seven brackets. The rates ranged from 1 percent on the first $20,000 of income to 7 percent on income exceeding $500,000.[20] I think many of us would love to go back to those days. It may be the worst amendment added to the Constitution, right before the Seventeenth. It wreaks havoc on our nation by turning us into a tax-and-spend federal government!

The Seventeenth Amendment simply changed the means for electing a senator. Originally, the Constitution had senators being elected by a state legislature. This amendment changed the election of senators to the vote of the people in each respective state. This forever changed the focus of the Senate from protecting the rights and interests of the states to whom they were accountable, to being another arm of the federal government that became obsessed with establishing MORE power at the federal level so they would be in charge of it. It's been a nightmare and anyone who has ever been a governor would likely love to see the Seventeenth Amendment repealed.

The Eighteenth Amendment was ratified in January of 1919, making alcohol illegal. The Roaring Twenties became the time of bootleggers and speakeasies. It is amazing that in our nation's history, activists who believed that a certain beverage had such an adverse effect on society and culture were able to convince political leaders to ban this substance, not by a law but by a Constitutional amendment. This amendment was repealed by the Twenty-First Amendment in 1933.

The Nineteenth Amendment gave women the right to vote in 1920.

The Twentieth Amendment relates to the end and beginning of presidential terms and also when Congress is to begin its session each year. The amendment also deals with presidential succession if a president-elect dies before assuming office.

The Twenty-Second Amendment restricted the terms of a president to two.

Amendments 23–27

The Twenty-Third Amendment gave the District of Columbia three electoral votes for presidential elections.

The Twenty-Fourth Amendment outlawed any poll tax being placed on a person that would prevent them from voting. This was a method used by some southern states to suppress the vote of the black community.

The Twenty-Fifth Amendment allows replacement of the president if he becomes unable to physically execute the duties of the office. Such a time could be temporary, e.g., if he were to have an operation and be under anesthesia, or suffer from a debilitating, non–life-threatening disease. This amendment was deemed necessary when it was learned that President Wilson had suffered a stroke, which was not immediately revealed. The amendment also sets the procedure for filling a vacancy in the office of vice president. The president nominates a person for the office of vice president and both houses of congress confirm by majority vote. President Nixon had to do this when his vice president resigned.

The Twenty-Sixth Amendment gave the right to vote to eighteen-year-olds. The reasoning was that if an eighteen-year-old could be drafted or could enlist in the military and put his or her life on the line, he or she should be able to vote.

The Twenty-Seventh Amendment, and the last to be ratified as of 1992, relates to compensation for those serving in Congress. It prohibits those in Congress from benefiting from any salary raise voted by them until after the next election.

The Constitution has served our nation well. Amendments are not easily to be executed and that was by design. Tweaking the nation by amendments was acceptable to the founders, but total transformation was not. Some on the political landscape today seek this transformation by taking aim at the Constitution.

9

Targeting the Constitution

★

The Founding Fathers gave us the Constitution to restrain the reach and power of a strong centralized federal government. The founders' intent is a major obstacle to the desires of the liberal Democrats who believe in and live for big government, so it is not a surprise liberals would take aim at altering the Constitution in a major way or replacing it altogether. There are two ways the liberal Left attacks the Constitution: one is to just ignore it and the other is to misinterpret it through the rulings of Supreme Court justices.

The Tenth Amendment, which was the last amendment in the Bill of Rights, clearly states that powers not given to the federal government belong to the states. The debate during the Constitutional Convention and during the ratification process focused on limited powers to the federal government and many powers to the state. This was to become reality in the following years. However, the liberal proponents of big government have chosen to ignore this amendment and forge ahead slowly and, whenever possible, to rapidly usurp more power in areas it has no business doing so. Let's look at three examples.

The Fed Reaches In

The federal government decided to get involved in the public school cafeteria. They passed the Healthy Hungry-Free Kids Act, which exists to provide lunches for schoolchildren, mostly those who are economically deprived. It now includes breakfast.[2] This may be a noble cause and in some places there may be a real need, but it simply is not the responsibility of the federal government. If a state wishes to enact such a program, it is well within their jurisdiction, but the Constitution does not give this concern to the federal government. Liberals love taking the federal government into this area because they then mike it for political gain, citing how much they care for hungry kids. We must remember that government lives by the golden rule, "If they provide the gold, they want to rule." Schools who take subsidies from the feds soon find that stipulations come with them, such as curriculum requirements. The liberals see the school as a place to feed a kid's tummy while they are feeding a kid's brain with liberal ideology mush.

When Michelle Obama was first lady, she wanted to get into the food and school issue. She said, "I think we can all agree that our classrooms should be healthy places where our kids are not bombarded with ads for junk food."[3] Yes, we all can agree on this, but according to the Constitution, it is not the business of the federal government to do anything about it. This is a concern for each state to address. The federal government is to be concerned with national defense, foreign trade, diplomatic relations, and the like, not setting menus in public schools. Her goals were noble and we can all agree that childhood obesity is a health risk to our nation's children, but do we want a bureaucrat in Washington determining the school lunch menu in every school in America?

The Vocational Educational Act of 1984, also known as the Perkins Act, provided funds for special populations (like those with disabilities and on public assistance) to have access to vocational training. Steve is very familiar with this act because he once worked as a job policy consultant for the Child and Family Services Department (Welfare) in Indiana, which was responsible for administering this law.[4] Again, the issue is, "Why is the federal government taking on vocational education?" This should be the responsibility of the states. Steve remembers he was a state employee administering a federal program. How does that line up with the Tenth Amendment?

The champion of federal violation of the Tenth Amendment is the Affordable Care Act, infamously known as Obamacare. In this law, Americans were required by government mandate to buy health care through the Obamacare website or some other means. The law was passed in 2012 when the House approved the Senate version of the bill. This had to be done or it would have never become law. After the senate voted, Scott Brown, a Republican, was voted in to fill the seat of the late Ted Kennedy, a Democrat. This meant there would no longer be a super majority of sixty senators in favor of the Democrats. Brown's vote meant that a Republican filibuster could prevent the bill from becoming law. The House had to take the Senate version as it was without any conference committee to hash out a new bill, which could incorporate ideas from both the House and the Senate. This would have created a new bill and Brown could then vote.

The question arose as to whether this mandate was a tax or not. It went to the Supreme Court and Chief Justice Roberts cast the deciding vote that deemed it a tax. The problem is that revenue laws must begin in the House, not the Senate, according to the Constitution Article I, Section 7. In December of 2018 US District Judge Reed O'Connor in Texas declared the Affordable Care Act unconstitutional, stating:

> The Individual Mandate can no longer be fairly read as an exercise of Congress's Tax Power and is still impermissible under the Interstate Commerce Clause—meaning the Individual Mandate is unconstitutional. The Individual Mandate is essential to and inseverable from the remainder of the ACA.[5]

The judge has a point. If the mandate is seen as a tax, it is unconstitutional because it started in the wrong house of Congress. The Supreme Court is bound to get another look at this legal matter. Given the purpose of the Tenth Amendment, the federal government does not have the power to get into the health care business. States can, but not the federal government.

The Left's Favorite Weapon

The favorite weapon of choice for the Left in attacking the Constitution is the Supreme Court justices. Liberals view the justices' rulings as the supreme loophole for advancing their agenda adverse to the original intent the founders had for the republic. Alexander Hamilton voiced in *Federalist Paper 78* his belief that the judiciary branch would be the least harmful to the rights protected in the Constitution:

> Whoever attentively considers the different departments of power must perceive, that, in a government in which they are separated from each other, the judiciary, from the nature of its functions, will always be the least dangerous to the political rights of the Constitution; because it will be least in a capacity to annoy or injure them.[6]

It is a shame that Hamilton's words are not a true description of our current political landscape. We Americans have suffered the loss of rights because of rulings by the Supreme Court, which would have dismayed the founders. The dangers posed by the justices of the Supreme Court were noted early on in our history. A delegate to the Constitutional Convention who remains virtually unknown to most Americans was Robert Yates, a representative from New York. He was an Anti-Federalist and opposed the Constitution by publishing essays in the *New York Journal,* which became known as the *Anti-Federalist Papers.*[7] He saw the problem the judiciary could be in the future. His warning is worthy of review:

> The real effect of this system of government, will therefore be brought home to the feelings of the people, through the medium of the judicial power. It is, moreover, of great importance, to examine with care the nature and extent of the judicial power, because those who are to be vested with it, are to be placed in a situation altogether unprecedented in a free country. They are to be rendered totally independent, both of the people and the legislature, both with respect to their offices and salaries. No errors they may commit can be corrected by any power above them, if any such power there may be, nor can they be removed from office for making ever so many erroneous adjudications.

> The only cause for which they can be displaced, is, conviction of treason, bribery, and high crimes and misdemeanors.

> This part of the plan is so modelled, as to authorize the

courts, not only to carry into execution the powers expressly given, but where are wanting or ambiguously expressed, to supply what is wanting by their own decisions.[8]

The independency of the judiciary was seen as a major problem because they were appointed for life and would not face constraint by the vote of the people or by check of the legislature. The president could check the legislature by a veto. The legislature could check the president by overriding his veto. There was no check or override of a Supreme Court decision. Their decisions would in effect become law that could be changed only by them in a later decision or by a constitutional amendment, which is very difficult to do. The power the Supreme Court has of determining, in a final decision, what is constitutional and unconstitutional is known as judicial review. It did not take long in our nation's life for this to be established, and it was all tied to party politics and not to the interest of the people.

The court case that ignited it all was *Marbury v. Madison*. Whole books have been written on this subject, but we will try to summarize it in a paragraph. Jefferson defeated incumbent John Adams in the 1800 election (even though it had to be determined in the House of Representatives). The two contending parties were the Federalists (Adams) and the Republicans (Jefferson). The Republicans were not like the Republicans of today. They were in essence anti-federalists or states' rights advocates.

Before leaving office, Adams signed the Judiciary Act of 1801. The Federalists had control of Congress but would lose it to their rivals when the new Congress was seated. The act set up sixteen federal circuit judgeships, done to give Federalists some hand of power. Jefferson instructed his Secretary of State, James Madison, not to deliver the commissions. One of these judges, William Marbury, filed suit. President Adams appointed his Secretary of State, John Marshall, as chief justice of the Supreme Court before he left the White House. Marshall wanted to make sure Marbury got his position and was instrumental in having the court establish that the high court had the power to decide on cases related to the constitutionality of laws passed by Congress and actions by the executive branch.[9]

Just how serious this was to our nation is seen in the words of Constitutional expert and esteemed author Mark Levin:

> Marshall's Federalist Party had lost the presidency and Congress, but Marshall was determined to fight back. And so the doctrine of judicial review was born. Yes, the Constitution is indeed the supreme law of the land, but now the Court, by its own fiat, would decide what is or is not constitutional. The Constitution's structure, including the balance of power between the three branches, was now broken.[10]

The Loophole

This judicial review has become the loophole for liberals to wreak havoc in our representative republic. This is why Supreme Court nominations are so important to liberals. When a liberal president chooses one, you can be sure that justice, when confirmed, will decide cases with the liberal agenda in mind. Now you can understand why the election of Donald Trump was so disturbing to liberals, because he could appoint justices to the Supreme Court with conservative values and views related to those of the founders. This is why the Kavanagh nomination evoked such desperate tactics from the Left as they tried to prevent his nomination with unprovable forty-year-old sex crime allegations.

Thomas Jefferson, the third president of the nation and also considered the founder of today's Democratic Party, was not shy about making his feelings known about the Supreme Court justices and the problems they posed for the nation with their independent position:

> At the establishment of our constitution, the judiciary bodies were supposed to be the most helpless and harmless members of the government. Experience, however, soon showed in what way they were to become the most dangerous; that the insufficiency of the means provided for their removal gave them a freehold and irresponsibility in office; that their decisions, seeming to concern individual suitors only, pass silent and unheeded by the public at large; that these decisions, nevertheless, become law by precedent, sapping, by little and little, the foundations of the constitution, and working its change by construction, before any one has perceived that that invisible and helpless worm has been busily employed in consuming its substance. In truth, man is not made to be trusted for life if secured against all liability to account.[11]

If Jefferson thought the worm was at work in his day, he would be astounded at what is taking place today. He also felt liberty was at risk.

> You seem . . . to consider the judges as the ultimate arbiters of all constitutional questions; a very dangerous doctrine indeed, and one which would place us under the despotism of an oligarchy. Our judges are as honest as other men, and not more

so . . . and their power [is] the more dangerous, as they are in office for life and not responsible, as the other functionaries are, to the elective control. The Constitution has erected no such single tribunal, knowing that to whatever hands confided, with corruptions of time and party, its members would become despots.[12]

The word "despotism" is a term that is averse to liberty and a free nation, but a man who drafted the Declaration of Independence and was once president feared the seed of tyranny was sown in the judiciary branch of our government.

In a letter to Abigail Adams, the wife of his political rival, John Adams, Jefferson wrote his belief that what the judges did in establishing judicial review was actually unconstitutional:

Nothing in the Constitution has given them [the federal judges] a right to decide for the Executive, more than to the Executive to decide for them. . . . The opinion which gives to the judges the right to decide what laws are constitutional and what not, not only for themselves, in their own sphere of action, but for the Legislature and Executive also in their spheres, would make the Judiciary a despotic branch.[13]

These words were written in 1804, when Jefferson was still president. He believed that this power of judicial review, of being the sole decider of what was constitutional and unconstitutional, was not something the Constitution gave the Supreme Court justices. A review of *The Federalist Papers* indicates Mr. Jefferson is correct. The debate at the Constitutional Convention clearly reveals the intent of having checks and balances on the various branches of government. The convention would never have accepted an unchecked judiciary, which would have no constraints on their actions either by the people or their elected representatives.

What has been done by the Supreme Court regarding the First Amendment as related to the religious clauses is atrocious. In chapter 3, the words of Joseph Story in 1833 were quoted, revealing that the original intent of the framers was to not have any particular sect or denomination be officially designated as the national church. This fact was reinforced by the Senate Judiciary Committee in 1853:

> The [First Amendment] clause speaks of "an establishment of religion." What is meant by that expression? It referred, without doubt, to that establishment which existed in the mother-country . . . endowment at the public expense, peculiar privileges to its members, or disadvantages or penalties upon those who should reject its doctrines or belong to other communities,— such law would be a "law respecting an establishment of religion. . . ."

> They intended, by this amendment, to prohibit "an establishment of religion" such as the English Church presented, or any thing like it. But they had no fear or jealousy of religion itself, nor did they wish to see us an irreligious people. . . .[14]

Later in the report it was stated:

> We are a Christian people . . . not because the law demands it, not to gain exclusive benefits or to avoid legal disabilities, but from choice and education; and in a land thus universally Christian, what is to be expected, what desired, but that we shall pay due regard to Christianity.[15]

If the concept of separation of church and state was a real thing for our founders, framers, and later government leaders, would these words have ever appeared in a report by a Senate Judiciary Committee? The answer is simple. They would not. Every time the Supreme Court issues a ruling detrimental to Christianity, it ignores the precedence established in our history. Precedence is valued and touted by liberal judges when it lines up with the liberal agenda. It is conveniently ignored when it does not, and no liberal judge worries about the complaints or disagreements because there is no recourse by people or legislature, thanks to the ill-founded doctrine of judicial review.

Let's examine some of the rulings that have been handed down by the high court regarding religion that totally ignore our founders' original intent:

> It is unconstitutional for students to start their school day with a nondenominational prayer. *Engel v. Vitale,* 1962.[16]

> It is unconstitutional to require students to read the Bible in school. *Abington School District v. Schemmp.* 1963.[17]

> If a student prays over his lunch, it is unconstitutional for him to pray aloud. *Reed v. Van Hoven,* 1965.[18]

> It is unconstitutional for a war memorial to be erected in the shape of a cross. *Lowe v. City of Eugene,* 1969.[19]

> It is unconstitutional for a public cemetery to have a planter in the shape of a cross, for if someone were to view that cross, it could cause "emotional distress" and thus constitute an "injury-in-fact." *Warsaw v. Tehachapi,* 1990.[20]

Even though the wording may be constitutionally acceptable,

a bill becomes unconstitutional if the legislator who introduced the bill had a religious activity in his mind when it was authored. *Wallace v. Jaffree,* 1985.[21]

It is unconstitutional for a classroom library to contain books that deal with Christianity or for a teacher to be seen with a personal copy of the Bible at school. *Roberts v. Madigan,* 1990.[22]

Artwork may not be displayed in schools if it depicts something religious, even if that artwork is considered a historic classic. *Washegesic v. Bloomingdale Public Schools,* 1994.[23]

It is unconstitutional for a kindergarten class to ask whose birthday is celebrated by Christmas. *Florey v. Sioux Falls School District,* 1980.[24]

How is it establishing a national church, like the Church of England or some other denomination, if a child prays over his school lunch out loud (*Reed v. Van Hoven*)? Is it establishing a national church for a school library to have books that deal with Christianity (*Roberts v. Madigan*)? Is this not censorship? Is not Christianity a religion and, at the very least, worthy of an academic study?

Aiming at the Second Amendment and Beyond

The Second Amendment is also a favorite target of the Left. After every unlawful mass shooting, they spring into gear clamoring for more gun control when time after time the person who did the shooting had to break existing law to commit the atrocious act. As this chapter was being written, the Democrat-controlled House of Representatives recently passed a new control bill that died in the Senate. According to the Constitution, the House has no business doing this. The Second Amendment contains the words "the right of the people to keep and bear Arms, shall not be infringed." Notice that it says "right of the people" and not right of the states. The founders reserved this right to the people. Also, it does not start by saying, "Congress shall not..." meaning this right is not to be infringed upon by any government entity. The right to bear arms is part of the Bill of Rights. This clearly shows the founders believed this right belongs to the people and is not to be removed by government. As we will see later when we examine the language of the Tenth Amendment, these two words are of course not identical: when the Constitution means "states," it says so.[25] In the case of *District of Columbia v. Heller* in 2008, the Supreme Court said the states and local governments have the right "to restrict and regulate firearms in a 'reasonable' manner."[26] A strong argument could be mounted that this decision by the high court was unconstitutional based on the Second Amendment, because people's rights were being infringed upon.

If the Left could have their way, American citizens would not have guns. Let's take a walk through history and see how the confiscation of arms has worked out for citizens around the world:

> In 1929, the Soviet Union established gun control. From 1929 to 1953, about 20 million dissidents, unable to defend themselves, were rounded up and exterminated. This doesn't include the 30 million "Uncle Joe" [Stalin] starved to death in the Ukraine.

> In 1911, Turkey established gun control. From 1915 to 1917, 1.5 million Armenians, unable to defend themselves, were rounded up and exterminated.

Germany established gun control in 1938 and from 1939 to 1945, leaving a populace unable to defend itself against the Gestapo and SS. Hundreds of thousands died as a result.

China established gun control in 1935. From 1948 to 1952, 20 million political dissidents, unable to defend themselves, were rounded up and exterminated.[27]

Colonists who had arms became a force with which the British had to contend. It is much easier to overwhelm and control a people when they do not have guns. Our founders knew this and that is the reason we have the Second Amendment.

In 1973 the Supreme Court ruled the state of Connecticut had to allow a noncitizen who was a Yale Law School graduate and married to a US citizen to take the state bar exam. This meant the state could not prevent noncitizens from practicing law. In dissent, Justice Warren Burger wrote, "The Constitution grants states the right to determine who is appropriate for representing the state in court, even if that should mean excluding anyone who isn't a US citizen."[28] You will recall the Tenth Amendment that gives states the rights not given to the federal government in the Constitution. Deciding who will take the state bar exam is not the concern of the federal government. Some other state could allow for a noncitizen to take the exam under certain circumstances. It is a state issue and not one where the federal government should have control.

Plyler v. Doe is an interesting case because it deals directly with illegal aliens. Illegals poured into a Texas border town and swamped the local school system. The school system refused to enroll the children of illegal aliens. A number of lawsuits were filed and the case made it to the Supreme Court. The court, based on the Fourteenth Amendment, ruled that the illegal alien children were covered as "persons" as provided in the amendment and were entitled to a free public education compliments of the taxpayers in the school district.[29]

The court even recognized that the Constitution does not demand a right to a free public education, but believed American society valued it so highly that it must be extended to illegal aliens' children.[30] When it was learned that a family was illegally in the country, why could not the school report them and have them deported? Why is our Supreme Court giving people who have broken the law by entering our country illegally an education and making the citizens of the community pay for it? Again, why is the federal government messing with a local school district? The Constitution does not give the federal government jurisdiction in local school districts.

Mark Levin asked the question in his book *Men in Black,* "Have you ever wondered how a federal government that is supposed to have limited power can now involve itself in essentially any aspect of our society?"[31] The answer, he says, is the commerce clause. This clause in found in the Constitution under Article I, Section 8: "To regulate commerce with foreign nations and among the several states." The Constitution was making the federal government the referee in economic activity. This clause was meant to expedite commercial dealings between the states, such as having only one currency instead of each state having its own. Like so many areas, the federal government began its slow creep to gain more centralized control in areas the founders never intended it to have.

In the 1930s, when FDR's New Deal was put in operation, the Supreme Court declared a number of its initiatives unconstitutional, believing they went beyond the powers given the federal government in the commerce section. However, in 1942, the case of *Wickard v. Filburn* started a trend that would see the court give the federal government more power as it related to commerce. Roscoe Filburn was a dairy farmer in Ohio who used a section of his land to plant wheat. He sold some of the wheat. He fed some to livestock, which he also sold. He ground a portion into flour and saved some for seed for the crop in the following year.

All of this activity occurred in the great state of Ohio. Therefore, there was no problem of any commerce violations because it was all taking place inside one state. That was not how the Supreme Court saw it. They said that he grew excess wheat beyond what the federal Agricultural Adjustment Act of 1938 allowed. This prevented him from having to buy wheat from outside sources, which could have been out of state.[32]

In the land of the free, farmer Filburn was not free to be self-sufficient in his farming operation. The federal government by way of the Supreme Court wanted to put him in a position where he would have to buy something from someone else. This is a power the federal government should never have. The commerce clause generated one of the favorite words of liberals: "regulate." Many regulations meant to protect have resulted in more harm than good as a large number of them, being of an absurd nature and illogical, have forced companies to lay off workers or even close down.

The Great Atrocity

The most anguishing action taken by the Supreme Court in its demonstration of unchecked power is in the case of *Roe v. Wade*, which made abortion legal. The court in essence made abortion the law of the land by acting more like a legislature than a judiciary entity. Mark Levin writes, "If you look in the Constitution, however, you will find no general 'right to privacy' any more than you will find a right to abortion—and for good reason: It's not there."[33] The right to privacy is what the court used to render a 7–2 decision to allow a woman to terminate the unborn child inside her. If having a right to privacy gives her the right to have an abortion, why would it not give her the right to operate a meth lab in her basement or engage in prostitution? Since the court based their ruling on the Fourteenth Amendment, let's review a part of it: "No State shall . . . deprive any person of life, liberty, or property, without due process of law; nor deny to any person within its jurisdiction the equal protection of the law."

The justice who received the main focus in the case was Harry Blackmun. He communicated his views on the right to privacy in writing:

> The Constitution does not explicitly mention any right of privacy. In a line of decisions, however . . . the Court has recognized that a right of personal privacy, or a guarantee of certain areas or zones of privacy, does exist under the Constitution. In varying contexts, the Court or individual Justices have, indeed, found at least the roots of that right in the First Amendment . . . in the Fourth and Fifth Amendments . . . in the penumbras of the Bill of Rights . . . or in the concept of liberty guaranteed by the first section of the Fourteenth Amendment. . . . These decisions make it clear that only personal rights that can be deemed "fundamental" or "implicit in the concept of ordered liberty" . . . are included in this guarantee of personal privacy. They also make it clear that the right has some extension to activities

relating to marriage . . . procreation . . . contraception . . . family
relationships . . . and child rearing and education . . . .[34]

The first line is of interest: "The Constitution does not explicitly
mention a right to Privacy." "However, just hang in there, liberals,
we justices will find it." The Constitution does not have the phrase
"separation of church and state," but somehow the court acts as if it
clearly exists and rules in conjunction with it.

The absurdity of this abortion ruling is the way in which the
Fourteenth Amendment is interpreted. Recall that this amendment
was ratified soon after the Civil War to give the free slaves full rights as
citizens. Using it with its "due process clause" to claim that the right to
privacy lies therein and make abortion law is indeed a stretch. But, what
matter? Once the decision is made it stands, since recourse is extremely
difficult and no justice will face removal.

It would be a fair argument that gun control should be ignored by
lawmakers since your firearm would be possessed in private. If I have the
right to privacy, how come the government wants to know how much I
make? The Supreme Court left its legal perch in *Roe v. Wade* and made
itself an expert in the medical field. It took upon itself to decide when
life begins or when personhood is achieved. The Constitution never
gave it this power. The personhood issue is important. In fact, Blackmun
even said that if personhood for the fetus was ever established, the case
for having an abortion would collapse.[35] There is much debate what real
impact this would have on making abortion illegal, but it sure could
affect public opinion and pose a political problem for liberals.

Two arguments strongly support the case for considering the fetus
a person. One is the fetus as a patient. Dr. Joseph Bruner pioneered this

amazing medical achievement at Vanderbilt University. A photograph from 1999 shows his latex-covered finger being touching the tiny hand of a twenty-two-week-old fetus who was suffering from spina bifida.[36] The operation was a success and the boy was able to live a healthy, normal life. The university continues to do wonders in this area of pre-birth surgery with fantastic results. So if a fetus can be a patient, why can't he or she be a person?

The other argument for personhood of the unborn is related to the criminal code of most states. Thirty states have laws recognizing "unborn children as victims throughout the period of prenatal development." Eight others give recognition for part of the prenatal development.[37] These laws consider it a homicide if a fetus dies when the mother is attacked. If a fetus can be a homicide victim, why can't he or she be a person?

The court ruling making abortion legal focused on the "due process clause" in the Fourteenth Amendment. The following statement proves ironic and reveals just how weak this ruling is from a legal perspective:

> The Court ignored the fact that dictionaries of the day defined "person" and "human being" interchangeably. It ignored the intentions of the Fourteenth Amendment's framers, like main author, John Bingham, who said the amendment protects "any human being" and is "universal." And the Court tried to dispute, unsuccessfully, the fact that both statutory laws and common-law history recognized unborn children as human beings deserving of protection. Most states at the time of the amendment literally classified abortion as an "offense against the person."[38]

William Rehnquist's dissent supports this concept: "To reach its result, the Court necessarily has had to find within the scope of the

Fourteenth Amendment a right that was apparently completely unknown to the drafters of the Amendment."[39] No matter how ridiculous the legal logic was that came into play, the nation was stuck with an atrocity that has resulted in over 60 million would-be Americans being killed between 1972 and 2019.

The Supreme Court has also proven to be the friend of pornography. From 1966 to 1970, the Supreme Court ruled on thirty-four decisions that favored pornographers.[40] The late Phyllis Schlafly was regarded by many as the "First Lady of Conservatism." She cited a very disturbing fact about a court ruling from 2003 in *U.S. v. American Library Association* related to pornography and public libraries:

> The Court nearly invalidated the Children's Internet Protection Act of 1999 based merely on the possibility that adult patrons of public library Internet terminals might be inconvenienced by having to ask a librarian to turn off the pornography filter installed to protect children. This decision assured adults that they can continue to enjoy pornography at taxpayers' expense at their local libraries.[41]

Churches are restricted from making politically supportive statements, or risk losing their nonprofit status (the Johnson Amendment).[42] Churches lose the right of free speech, but pornographers, with liberal activist judges on the Supreme Court, have an open highway to pedal their obscene merchandise. It now is possible for a nine-year-old to download a hardcore porn film to his smart phone in thirty seconds.

How to Correct

The judiciary branch needs to be reformed so that it is more in line with the spirit of the Constitution where real checks and balances are the norm. It would take an amendment to the Constitution for this to take place. Amendments are difficult to execute, and since the liberals see the judiciary branch as a loophole to benefit their agenda, they will always stand opposed to any change. Mark Levin wrote a book entitled *The Liberty Amendments* in which he proposes a number of dream amendments to help restore the American Republic. The one related to the Supreme Court is ideal for the current situation we are dealing with. It is worthy of review to cultivate our hope:

An Amendment to Establish Term Limits for Supreme Court Justices and Super-Majority Legislative Override

SECTION 1: No person may serve as Chief Justice or Associate Justice of the Supreme Court for more than a combined total of twelve years.

SECTION 2: Immediately upon ratification of this Amendment, Congress will organize the justices of the Supreme Court as equally as possible into three classes, with the justices assigned to each class in reverse seniority order, with the most senior justices in the earliest classes. The terms of office for the justices in the First Class will expire at the end of the fourth Year following the ratification of this Amendment, the terms for the justices of the Second Class will expire at the end of the eighth Year, and of the Third Class at the end of the twelfth Year, so that one-third

229

of the justices may be chosen every fourth Year.

SECTION 3: When a vacancy occurs in the Supreme Court, the President shall nominate a new justice who, with the approval of a majority of the Senate, shall serve the remainder of the unexpired term. Justices who fill a vacancy for longer than half of an unexpired term may not be renominated to a full term.

SECTION 4: Upon three-fifths vote of the House of Representatives and the Senate, Congress may override a majority opinion rendered by the Supreme Court.

SECTION 5: The Congressional override under Section 4 is not subject to a Presidential veto and shall not be the subject of litigation or review in any Federal or State court.

SECTION 6: Upon three-fifths vote of the several state legislatures, the States may override a majority opinion rendered by the Supreme Court.

SECTION 7: The States' override under Section 6 shall not be subject of litigation or review in any Federal or State court, or oversight or interference by Congress or the President.

SECTION 8: Congressional or State override authority under Sections 4 and 6 must be exercised no later than twenty-four months from the date of the Supreme Court rendering its majority opinion, after which date Congress and the States are prohibited from exercising the override.[42]

This amendment would be a great addition to the Constitution, but we must face reality. It is not likely to happen. Our best current check on the Supreme Court is not to vote for a Democrat for president or the senate so liberal justices cannot be appointed.

10

The Threatening C: Corruption

★

We have looked at the three Cs that have made America great, but there is another C that threatens these three essential items and the welfare and prosperity of the nation. That C is Corruption. When you look up the word "corruption" in a thesaurus you will find these words among the listed synonyms: bribery, crookedness, dishonesty, doctoring, evil, falsification, fraud, graft, immorality, profiteering, shadiness, unscrupulousness, vice, and viciousness.[1] These are all things that have no place in a government that is to exist for "We the people" in a free representative republic. The reality is they abound and do so to the detriment of us the people. Corruption touches both of our major political parties. If corruption were a swimming pool, the Republicans would be up to their knees in the shallow end, while the Democrats would seek out the deepest end and head for the bottom.

The topic of corruption in politics has whole books dedicated to it. Michelle Malkin actually wrote three hundred pages focused just on corruption in the Obama administration. This chapter will provide a brief look at some examples of corruption that have or are still affecting our nation. The first example is close to home because it is related to

Steve's former representative, Bob Ney. Mr. Ney, a Republican from Ohio, was sentenced to thirty months in prison for accepting bribes of luxury vacation trips, skybox seats at sporting events, and campaign contributions from Jack Abramoff, who was guilty of scandal involving wire fraud and a boat casino in Florida.[2] Abramoff was an unscrupulous lobbyist who was sentenced to four years in prison for corruption. Abramoff also touched Democrats when he convinced Harry Reid to send a letter that would help a client of Abramoff's, a Native American tribe, to win over a competing tribe for a casino. Contributions were made from Abramoff connections to Reid's campaign, but no charges were brought.[3] Ney's corruption cost the Republicans the congressional seat for the next two elections.

The Obama Stimulus Bill

When President Obama took office, one of his first items of business was the so-called Stimulus Bill. It was actually called the American Recovery and Reinvestment Act (ARRA), which came about in February 2009. It was to add nearly $800 billion into the economy in many places where there were to be "shovel ready jobs." As to whether this program had an overall positive effect on the nation's economy or not is a matter of debate, but one thing is for sure, it had its corruption. The company Solyndra is an example. This California-based solar panel manufacturer secured a $535 million loan from the Obama stimulus program (ABBA). Note the following news report:

> ABC News discovered that the solar-tech firm Solyndra got unusually low interest rates on its federally-guaranteed loans before it collapsed last month, sending 1000 workers

to the unemployment line in California. Other green-tech firms receiving loans paid as much as three and four times the interest rate Solyndra secured for its $535 million from Barack Obama's 2009 stimulus bill from the Treasury's Federal Financing Bank. ABC notes that other green-tech firms didn't have the connections that Solyndra had to Obama.[4]

It seems that favoritism was afoot. When Solyndra first tried for a loan during the Bush administration, Dun & Bradsteet only gave it a fair rating. When Obama came to office, the Solyndra application was fast-tracked through and also got a super loan interest rate of 1.025 percent, far lower than other green-energy companies received. Could it have been because Solyndra's foremost investor was Oklahoma billionaire George Kaiser, who happened to be a campaign finance bundler for Obama? Of course, when Solyndra went bankrupt, the investors got paid off first instead of the taxpayers.[5]

As money was distributed from this program, a pattern of corruption appeared. Fox News reported:

> The stimulus money may have failed to go to the states the president promised, but a clear pattern does emerge. Stimulus dollars were highly correlated to which political party controlled the state: Having an entirely Democrat congressional delegation in 2009, when the bill passed, increases the per capita stimulus dollars that the state receives per person by $460. In addition, the states that Obama won by largest percentage margin in 2008 got most of the money.[6]

Many other stories reveal that much of this money went to pay off entities or organizations, including unions, that helped Obama get elected. This is a corrupt use of tax dollars. One of the first big encounters of corruption for the Obama administration was an operation called "Fast and Furious." It started in November of 2009 in the Phoenix office of Alcohol, Tobacco, Firearms, and Explosive. Gun buyers were allowed to take firearms bought in the US into Mexico. Many of these buyers were suspected criminals. The plan was to track the weapons once they were sold to powerful drug cartels. Whistleblowers and investigators' efforts found there were no attempts to trace the guns.[7] One of these guns was used in the killing of border guard Brian Terry. Some two thousand guns are believed to have ended up in the hands of drug trafficking criminals. When this matter was under investigation by Congress, the White House halted emails being sent to Congress claiming executive privilege. This actually led to Obama's Attorney General Eric Holder receiving contempt of Congress charges in 2012. It has been discovered that the real motive of the operation by the administration was to foster evidence for more control.[8] This is corruption.

IRS Chooses Sides

One of the major corrupt incidents of the Obama administration was the IRS scandal. It was connected to the Tea Party Movement. After Obama implemented policies of higher taxes and increasing debt, there was adverse reaction at the grassroots level as various groups organized to oppose these policies and became politically active. They used the name "Tea Party" after the rebellious colonists who executed the famed "Boston Tea Party" of dumping British tea into the Boston harbor protesting the high tax on it prior to the Revolutionary War. These groups were very active and effective in helping the Republicans win back control of the House of Representatives in 2010. The presidential election was coming up in 2012 and these groups were increasing and expanding their efforts, leading many of them to seek nonprofit organization status by application to the Internal Revenue Service (IRS).

The groups did not receive their status in a timely matter. Lois Lerner of the IRS was in charge of this area in the agency and appeared before the Republican-controlled House Oversight Committee. She made a long statement as to why she was innocent of any wrongdoing and then immediately refused to answer any questions based on her right from the Fifth Amendment. This caused quite a stir because one who comes to testify does not make a statement and then refuse to answer questions. The Fifth Amendment is to be claimed without prior comments. Logic would suggest that if you are indeed innocent of any wrongdoing, then there would be no way you could incriminate yourself by answering questions.

When Obama was pressed about the IRS scandal in an interview by Bill O'Reilly on Super Bowl Sunday 2014, he responded that there was "not even a smidgen of corruption."[9]

The IRS scandal in October 2017 has been put to rest by the Department of Justice by a statement from then Attorney General Jeff Sessions. In the statement, he said that conservative groups were singled out far more than others and that these groups had to provide the IRS with sensitive information that even related to the groups' donors, all of which was not needed by the IRS. He went on to admonish the actions of the IRS in this wrongdoing:

> The IRS's use of these criteria as a basis for heightened scrutiny was wrong and should never have occurred. It is improper for

the IRS to single out groups for different treatment based on their names or ideological positions. Any entitlement to tax exemption should be based on the activities of the organization and whether they fulfill requirements of the law, not the policy positions adopted by members or the name chosen to reflect those views.

There is no excuse for this conduct. Hundreds of organizations were affected by these actions, and they deserve an apology from the IRS. We hope that today's settlement makes clear that this abuse of power will not be tolerated.[10]

The word "smidgen" means bit or particle, something really small. It does not appear something small was going on with the IRS. The fundraising efforts of the conservative Tea Party groups were stymied, preventing them from being the force they wanted to be in the 2012 election in which they desired to unseat Obama. No one from the IRS was indicted and Lois Lerner retired with her pension intact. The IRS scandal was major corruption, but it was also successful as far as Democrats were concerned. The Tea Party folks' voices were at a lower volume during the 2012 campaign, and none of the liberals involved had to take a fall. It was corruption to be sure, but just another successful day at the office for the Democrats.

Islamic Votes at a High Cost

Democrats desire the power. They get it by winning elections. The way they win elections is by stringing together a coalition of voting blocs. Their strategy is to find new voting blocs, maintain old ones, and shrink the voting blocs of their opponents. One voting bloc the

Democrats are very interested in led to another Obama administration scandal. The voting bloc is Islamic-American citizens and the scandal, Benghazi. Islamic Americans will outnumber Jews as voters in the US by 2040.[11] This means that a substantial number of Muslims now vote. The Democrats want this voting bloc and aim to cultivate it for future elections. This explains why there was a ban on the term "Islamic extremists" in the Obama Administration.[12]

In 2012 there was a coordinated attack on the US consulate in Benghazi, Libya, by Islamic terrorists, which resulted in the deaths of four Americans, including the ambassador to Libya, Christopher Stevens. The attack happened fifty-six days before the presidential election. This presented a problem for the Obama reelection campaign. The president was basking in the glory of having killed Osama bin Laden and was using it as a signal that al-Qaeda was virtually defeated. If this assault in Benghazi could be proven to be the work of organized terrorists, it would hurt the proclaimed narrative. Obama's team, which included Hillary Clinton, then secretary of state, set out to sell something different than a terrorist attack. They called it a protest against an anti-Muslim video made in the US by someone who was against Islam. Susan Rice, the ambassador to the UN, was trotted out to lie on all the Sunday news shows, pushing the video excuse. The thing is, protesters don't bring grenade launchers to protests. Four brave Americans from the CIA headquarters in Benghazi came to the aid of some thirty-plus Americans trapped in the consulate. Two of those men lost their lives. The two heroes who survived gave accounts of how sophisticated the attack was and how heavily armed the terrorists were.[13]

The corruption did not stop there. Obama and Clinton

commissioned a video advertisement, using seventy thousand dollars of taxpayers' money aimed for a broadcast in Pakistan for appeasing any offended would-be terrorists.[14] Usually scandals end up costing the nation money. Obama's Fast and Furious and Benghazi cost America not only money but also five lives. Obama and his team were sending a loud and clear message to Muslim voters, "We haven't forgotten you, and we stand against those who defame your faith," even if they would dare call protesters armed like an army terrorists. This is corruption in the highest degree.

"You Can Keep Your Doctor"—NOT

Let's look at the crowning jewel of Obama's corrupt scandals, which can be none other than Obamacare. Democrats like to call it by its congressional name, The Affordable Care Act. We all remember those oft-spoken words of Obama, "If you like your doctor, you can keep your doctor. If you like your plan, you can keep your plan." He also said that on average every household would save $2,500 on medical insurance payments. All of this was not true and most found their payments going higher. Some had very few choices as to what health care plan they could buy into. Obamacare was a scam from the beginning. One might have thought that the House speaker at the time, Nancy Pelosi, was not smart. Then she made a statement that removed all doubt: "We have to pass the bill to find out what's in it."[15] Doesn't it seem logical that before a congressperson would vote on a bill, they would want to read it and know what was in it? The real evidence of corruption for Obamacare came from one of the brains who was solicited to help draft and promote it.

Katie Pavlich wrote an excellent article for *Townhall* that exposes the untruthful Jonathan Gruber, an MIT professor who was one of the architects of the Obamacare plan and admits to lying about it. Gruber actually boasted about lying to the American people to get the bill passed. Ms. Pavlich's article refers to a released video that had Gruber's comments about purposely preventing transparency to the American people:

> "You can't do it politically, you just literally cannot do it. Transparent financing and also transparent spending. I mean, this bill was written in a tortured way to make sure CBO did not score the mandate as taxes. If CBO scored the mandate as taxes the bill dies. Okay? So it's written to do that," Gruber said. "In terms of risk rated subsidies, if you had a law which said that healthy people are going to pay in, you made explicit healthy people pay in and sick people get money, it would not have passed. Lack of transparency is a huge political advantage. And basically, call it the stupidity of the American voter or whatever, but basically that was really critical to get for the thing to pass. Look, I wish Mark was right that we could make it all transparent, but I'd rather have this law than not."[16]

Pavlich goes on to cite four points that Gruber's statement reveals:

1. Lying to the American people is justified by the Obama administration, proving they believe in the "ends justify the means."

2. Lack of transparency is a political advantage in the short run, but voters remember in the long run.

3. Insulting Americans by calling them stupid and purposely deceiving them is despicable and will hurt a party politically at election time.

4. Obamacare was sold on lies. It was drafted not to be a tax but had to be argued that way to save it at the Supreme Court.[17]

As has been pointed out earlier, tax legislation has to originate in the House, and Obamacare began in the Senate. The bill is basically unconstitutional and a product of intentional corruption. Obamacare is just one step toward trying to get Medicare for all, which the Democrats hope will make us all one voting bloc that will always vote for them to keep our health care.

Republicans also got some corruption experience regarding Obamacare. Trump became president and a Republican majority in the House and Senate had the opportunity to repeal Obamacare.[18] During the campaign some of these senators promised their voters they would vote to repeal Obamacare. In fact, more than once, the Republican-controlled Congress voted to repeal it, only to have then President Obama veto the bill. These were called "Show Votes" since they knew the veto was coming. When their vote would have truly counted, three senators would not stand with the American people who wanted it repealed. When you will not be true to what you promised your constituents, that is corruption.

Democrats would love to have their big government run a one-payer national healthcare system and seek to make us all one big voting bloc, claiming not voting for them is voting to end your health care. Our health is too important to become a political football. A billboard campaign in Ireland had a picture of a hospital gurney. The ad gave the name of the candidate with his promise, "I will shorten Gurney Lines." The message was clear. National health care was inefficient and elective surgeries had long waits. The customer service was poor. We don't need that in the United States.

War on Poverty or on the Poor?

One of the longest running acts of corruption promoted and championed by the Democrats is the War on Poverty. The title sounds so noble. Who would not want to help the poor? But the Democrats don't help the poor, they exploit the poor. They have used the so-called War on Poverty to construct a voting bloc that they maintain at taxpayers' expense. The War on Poverty was part of President Lyndon Johnson's Great Society sweeping welfare program. Johnson's intentions were admirable; he wanted to ease the pain of poverty in the short term by helping people acquire self-sufficient skills that hopefully would end poverty altogether.[19] Johnson saw it as an investment that would pay off in the elimination of poverty, allowing spending on related programs to end. When a Democrat talks about "investment," you'd best be ready to hold on to your wallet. Johnson's vision did not become a reality. The welfare program aimed at re-leveling poverty has perpetuated down through the years. Democrat welfare programs become money pits that never get filled.

The War on Poverty has resulted in some $15 trillion dollars in expenditures with very disappointing results. It has been reported the government spent $20,610 on every poor person and $61,830 per poor family in 2012.[20] From 1950 to 1970, self-sufficiency improved strongly. The War on Poverty began in 1964, and from 1970 to the present self-sufficiency has shown no positive progress and basically has come to a halt. The self-sufficiency rate has become static, poverty rates don't improve, but the money continues to be spent.[21] The following statement from The Heritage Foundation provides revealing insight on the failure of the welfare program:

> This lack of progress in building self-sufficiency is due in major part to the welfare system itself. Welfare wages war on social capital, breaking down the habits and norms that lead to self-reliance, especially those of marriage and work. It thereby generates a pattern of increasing intergenerational dependence. The welfare state is self-perpetuating: By undermining productive social norms, welfare creates a need for even greater assistance in the future.

> As the War on Poverty passes the half-century mark, it is time to rein in the endless growth in welfare spending and return to LBJ's original goals. As the economy improves, total means-tested spending should be moved gradually toward pre-recession levels. Able-bodied, non-elderly adult recipients in all federal welfare programs should be required to work, prepare for work, or at least look for a job as a condition of receiving benefits.

> Finally—and most important—the anti-marriage penalties should be removed from welfare programs, and long-term steps should be taken to rebuild the family in lower-income communities.[22]

The anti-marriage penalties merit attention. It can be argued that the black nuclear family has been destroyed by the War on Poverty. In 1964 close to 75 percent of black children were born into homes where both parents were present. In 2008 72 percent of black babies were born to unwed mothers. This is twice the number experienced among whites.[23]

The Democrats like to proclaim themselves the all-caring advocates of the black community. The War on Poverty actually has been detrimental to blacks who saw no real economic improvement to their lives until President Trump's tax reform led to the lowest unemployment rate for blacks in years. Democrats love to portray people in poverty as victims. They are poor because rich people made them that way. There are basically four ways a person goes into poverty. One is to quit high school before graduation. The second is to have a child out of wedlock. The third is to be busted for committing a crime. Lastly is making bad decisions that affect one's life, such as becoming addicted to drugs or alcohol. No business person we know has advised someone to quit school, have premarital sex, commit a crime, or become addicted to a substance. A lot of poverty is the result of one's personal choice. This is not true in all cases, but it is in far too many.

Some pronounce the War on Poverty a failure due to the amount spent with low increase in self-sufficiency. However, the Democrats consider it a fantastic success because it helped to create a voting bloc of black voters, which the Left has gone to great pains to maintain and grow with our tax dollars. This is corruption.

The liberals are so concerned about maintaining control of this voting group it has led to their taking some absurd positions regarding law enforcement. The shooting of Michael Brown in Ferguson, Missouri, is a prime example. This incident revealed double corruption. There was corruption by the liberal-biased news media rushing to judgment by condemning the white police officer who shot Brown; and there were liberal Leftists crying about the injustice done to the poor young man who was wrongly gunned down by a racist cop. Michael Brown had left a convenience store where he shoplifted some cigarillos and even pushed the store clerk. Officer Darren Wilson later encountered Brown on a street where the officer and Brown had an altercation that ended in Brown being fatally shot. The story first reported was that Brown put up his hands and said, "Don't shoot." At this account, rioting took place as blacks in the community protested their outrage in violent ways. The liberal news media did its best to highlight this view of the story. After a thorough investigation, it was learned that Brown went after Officer Wilson in his squad car and tried to take his gun. Fearing for his life, Wilson shot Brown. Wilson was cleared by a grand jury.[24]

The investigation that cleared Wilson did not stop the group called Black Lives Matter from cranking into gear to protest, with one of their loudest voices being Rev. Al Sharpton. On December 13, 2014, thousands of protestors marched in New York City chanting "What do we want?" And the answer came back, "Dead cops!" Al Sharpton called for marches across the country and was himself in DC conducting a march while the one in New York City was happening.[25]

A week later, the protestors got their dead cops. Ismaaiyl Brinsley came to New York from Baltimore and fatally shot officers Wenjian Liu and Rafael Ramos as they sat in their patrol car. The shooter later killed himself as police closed in on him at a subway platform.[26] Al Sharpton went strangely quiet. Perhaps he was spending time working on a way to pay off the millions of dollars he still owes in income taxes. If the forces on the Left could have unfairly concocted Officer Wilson as guilty of homicide in Ferguson, they would have done so and lost no sleep.

Their friends in the media would have been glad to help. Corruption was in play, but it did not prevail. However, two policemen lost their lives, which likely would not have happened if biased coverage and protests, which had no basis for being conducted, had not happened.

Media—Only News to Help the Blue

The liberal news media, which includes CNN, MSNBC, NBC, ABC, CBS, *The New York Times, The Washington Post*, and a host of other outlets, got the Ferguson story wrong but many others followed. The liberal media is really not news media at all because it does not seek to report the truth. Its mission is to present information to advance the Democratic liberal agenda. They are not real journalists, but Democratic political operatives dedicated to the liberal agenda. If a story can be spun in such a way to hurt a conservative, that is how it will be presented. If a story can help the liberal cause, then it will receive major focus. If the story would hurt a liberal, the solution is easy: just ignore it. When Obama saw the unemployment rate go below 8 percent, it was big positive news. Donald Trump got the unemployment below 4 percent and you are lucky to hear a peep about it in the liberal media.

Rich Noyes, director of research for the Media Research Center, said, "As the Media Research Center has been documenting all year, the media have approached the Trump presidency with unrelenting hostility."[27] He went on to say, "Even as the media whine about Trump, their hostile coverage shows no let up. Our study of news in June, July, and August found an identical rate of 91 percent negative coverage—which means TV news is unchanged in its hostility toward the president."[28] Lara Logan, who was a foreign correspondent for

60 Minutes on CBS, revealed that the liberal media cited above is "absurdly left wing" and has a Democratic bias.[29] This was hardly a major scoop. Just a casual glance at this media and one would get this impression. Bernard Goldberg, a former reporter for CBS, wrote a book entitled *Bias* in which he documents how the so-called mainstream media distorts the news in favor of liberals.[30]

There are a number of examples I could present that prove the bias and disingenuousness of the mainstream, liberal media. The one that is paramount happened during the writing of this book. It is the news story about the Covington, Kentucky, kid, Nicholas Sandmann, who was in Washington, DC, for the March for Life in January of 2019. He and some other students in his group were given MAGA (Make America Great Again) hats. As they calmly stood waiting for a bus to pick them up, Native American activist Nathan Phillips came over to Nicolas and stood a short distance from him, beating his drum and chanting. Nicholas stood his ground and simply smiled back. The following words single out how NBC dealt with the story, which was matched by many other sources.

> It [NBC] was the first of the broadcast networks to jump on the story, without having all the facts. On Saturday's *NBC Nightly News*, anchor Jose Diaz-Balart immediately accepted leftist viral online reaction as the truth, proclaiming: "A troubling scene many are calling racist, played out in Washington yesterday, on the steps of the Lincoln Memorial. Some students harassing an older Native American, of yet a Vietnam vet in the midst of a special ceremony." Not only did NBC fail to retract the story the next day, but on Monday's *Nightly News*, reporter Ron

Allen continued touting claims of "racism" against the teens. It wasn't until Tuesday's *Today* show that the network started to acknowledge that "these videos should be a lesson in not rushing to judgment.[31]

The fact is that many prominent news outlets did rush to judgment. Some even accused the boy in question of weaponizing a smirk. Other videos clearly showed that a group of radical blacks known as the Black Hebrew Israelites initiated the contention by yelling derogatory and obscene remarks at the Covington kids while Phillips was seen walking directly over to Nicholas to single him out as a target of his protest.

The Sandmann family has hired famous attorney Lin Wood to sue many of the media outlets for as much $250,000 each for ruining the reputation of the teenager. There was one reason why the news outlets jumped to judgment. It was a chance to make Donald Trump look bad. The kids were wearing MAGA hats and it looked like a great opportunity to paint Trump supporters as racial bigots, but instead they were the victims. Fake news rides again and it is corrupt.

The integrity of climate change information and predictions has already been touched on in a previous chapter. Climate change is used by the Left to expand their control as they seek more power in big government-run programs. If they can get people to believe that climate change (global warming) is real, it will be easier to have them agree to pay higher taxes to prevent it, and be willing to accept a lower standard of living to lessen a carbon footprint. There were eighteen predictions made around 1970 about climate change that have not come true. Below are a few of them, all of which were proven wrong:

Population will inevitably and completely outstrip whatever

small increases in food supplies we make," Paul Ehrlich confidently declared in the April 1970 issue of *Mademoiselle*. "The death rate will increase until at least 100–200 million people per year will be starving to death during the next ten years."

Ehrlich sketched out his most alarmist scenario for the 1970 Earth Day issue of *The Progressive*, assuring readers that between 1980 and 1989, some 4 billion people, including 65 million Americans, would perish in the "Great Die-Off."

In January 1970, *Life* reported, "Scientists have solid experimental and theoretical evidence to support . . . the following predictions: In a decade, urban dwellers will have to wear gas masks to survive air pollution . . . by 1985 air pollution will have reduced the amount of sunlight reaching earth by one half. . . .

Paul Ehrlich chimed in, predicting in 1970 that "air pollution . . . is certainly going to take hundreds of thousands of lives in the next few years alone." Ehrlich sketched a scenario in which 200,000 Americans would die in 1973 during "smog disasters" in New York and Los Angeles.

Ecologist Kenneth Watt declared, "By the year 2000, if present trends continue, we will be using up crude oil at such a rate... that there won't be any more crude oil. You'll drive up to the pump and say, 'Fill 'er up, buddy,' and he'll say, 'I am very sorry, there isn't any."[32]

If these smart people were so sure about their predictions, which turned out to be wrong, then why should we believe their present-day forecasts? One of the key items that climate change alarmists like to point to is rising sea levels, which they believe are due to the ice caps melting. The problem is that the Arctic ice field actually grew in 2017.[33] In Alaska, there is an area where many hopeful prospectors climbed up a mountain pass to get over to Yukon where gold was discovered. There was a picture of a long line of men ascending the pass, which was free of snow. A visit there in June found there was snow on the pass. If one asked a guide about global warming and shouldn't the ground now be without snow, the answer was that glaciers can grow and recede over time, which is a very natural process and there is nothing we can do about it.

Liberals blame conservatives and want them to feel guilty about the use of fossil fuels and our high standard of living. If we are to listen to Alexandria Ocasio-Cortez and her Green New Deal, we should be willing to stop using fossil fuels, stopping eating beef (because cows must be eliminated to end their dangerous polluting flatulence), and say goodbye to airplanes so the skies will not be marred by fossil fuel exhaust. I wonder if Ocasio-Cortez knows that her lipstick is made from petroleum (a fossil fuel). Plastics are manufactured using petroleum. Just think of all the convenient products made with plastics. The mobile phone might become a bit heavy if plastics cannot be made because of the New Green Deal, not to mention a million other products. One thing is for sure, the sacrifices we will be asked to make to curb climate change will not be required of the ruling class who will levy them. This is corruption.

Elections: Anything to Win

One area in which liberal Democrats excel in corruption is elections. Some Democrats have been shown to lie, cheat, or commit voter fraud to win an election. Power is the goal and they must win elections to get that power. California has an open primary, which means you can vote for any candidate from any party. The two highest vote getters oppose each other in the November election. The Senate race of 2018 had two Democrats running against each other. This guaranteed the Senate seat would stay with the Democrats, and it prevented a Republican challenger from providing a truly opposing voice and an opportunity to gain exposure for future races.

Early voting is now allowed in many states, giving parties more time to get voters to the polls but also allowing for more opportunities for voter fraud. Philadelphia is a Democrat-run city. It has had over 100 percent of registered voters casting ballots in a precinct. This is obviously voter fraud, but since Democrats are in control, there is no accountablilty.[34]

Another questionable factor in elections is "provisional ballots." The following statement reveals how it works in Tennessee:

> Provisional votes are cast on hand-marked paper ballots, sealed with affidavits and voter registration forms for a provisional counting board made up of two Democrats and two Republicans to determine their validity. The paper ballots are used in cases where someone claims to be a registered voter but is not on the electronic poll book of all voters in the county and/or didn't have the photo identification required by Tennessee law to vote.[35]

Notice it says, ". . . ballots are used in cases where someone claims to be registered but is not on the electronic poll book . . . ." It seems like it would be rather easy to have all legal registered voters on the roll. I'm sure that everyone with a driver's license is registered and in a computer file. Why not so with voters? Provisional ballots are a creative way to get more votes, which are overwhelmingly cast by Democratic voters.[36]

The Democrat-controlled House of Representatives passed a voting bill that had an amendment that considered lowering the voting age to sixteen and also allowing illegals to vote in local elections.[37] This bill will not see the light of day in the Senate, but it reveals what's on the liberal wish list. If illegals got the vote on the local level, it would only be a matter of time till they advocated for national elections. Having sixteen-year-olds voting would expand the voting bloc of the Democrats, since they control public education where more attention is given to liberal indoctrination than education. The Democrats are always seeking ways to make election laws favor them to where one day elections will be purely academic, as they will always win. This is corruption.

One can see why the Democrats advocate for open borders. They see it as a means of future voter recruitment. The adjective "future" in some cases could be changed to "present." Democrat-run counties and precincts in California and elsewhere engage in practices so lenient at the polls that many illegals end up voting. The following statement provides incriminating evidence that illegals are voting as authorities look the other way:

> In practice, none of these so-called safeguards is functioning correctly. Based on voting history records, large numbers of ineligible aliens are registering to vote and casting ballots.

They are canceling out the valid votes of American citizens. In some Virginia jurisdictions, the number of people registered to vote exceeds the number of citizens eligible to vote. When the Justice Department has been told of aliens registering to vote and committing federal felonies, nothing is done.[38]

The Justice Department alluded to here was the Obama Justice Department since this statement is from a report written before the 2016 election. Now we see why liberal Democrats want an open border with Mexico. It is a pipeline for importing voters for Democrats. Those coming into the country illegally are mostly unskilled and likely to want to partake of social benefit programs from the American welfare system. When they vote, they know what party advocates the handouts and even makes them possible to illegals.

The illegals coming into our country from the southern border pose a host of problems. It is estimated that 90 percent of the heroin coming into the United States comes from Mexico.[39] Non-Mexicans, some of whom are terrorists, have entered the US from the southern border.[40] Many of the girls and women brought into the country illegally are forced into sex trafficking.[41] Illegals are involved in violent crime and kill many Americans.[42] Drugs, terrorists, sex trafficking, and criminal acts including murder are pouring into our country, but Democrats are fine with it all because it is outweighed by more voters for them. The young people who die from an overdose of fentanyl-laced heroin, and those murdered by illegals or killed by illegals driving drunk are just collateral damage in the Democratic political war against Republicans. Democrats in the ruling class know they are safe in their gated communities or wall-secured homes. Liberals don't want a wall at the south border because they benefit from the corruption that an open border allows.

Corruption is even found in the Obama-run college student loan program. Obama encouraged efforts to have the government take over the operation of student loans. It is estimated that in 2015 the student loan deficit was $22 billion. Policies operated by the Obama administration showed generosity to borrowers. More students who were high risk for not repaying their loan received loans, which resulted in increasing the nation's debt.[43] However, I am sure that those students who got these loans were happy to vote Democrat in the following election. Once again, we the taxpayers end up paying for helping the Democrats placate one of their voting blocs.

Tale of Two Policies

During the election campaign of 2016, Hilary Clinton admitted that she would govern corruptly if elected and it virtually went under the radar. Clinton told executives in the banking industry she has a public policy and a private policy on Wall Street reform.[44] Let me translate this. What Mrs. Clinton was telling the investment bankers of Wall Street was, "I am going to have to beat on you guys in the campaign so it looks like I have you as a target. This will get me votes from those who are suspect of Wall Street rich people. Rest assured that when I take office, I will not deliver on dinging you guys making millions on Wall Street so you can donate to my campaign without worry. I'll give the public some excuse that obstructive Republicans or complicated red tape is hindering me, but I am working hard to make major changes in this area." This was premeditated corruption.

Slush Fund for Sex

Another mind-boggling story of corruption is related to members of Congress. Congress has had a slush fund to pay off sexual harassment cases of which members of Congress from either party have been accused. The payout amount has reached $17 million. What a wonderful way to spend our tax dollars. In the private sector, people lose their jobs for this wrongful action. Why do congressmen get a pass and use our money to do so?[45]

The Russian Hoax

The Mount Everest of corruption in our government happened in the election of 2016 and the first two years of the Trump presidency. It is best entitled the same as the provocative book by Gregg Jarrett, *The Russia Hoax*. It is the biggest scandal in America's history that amounted to an attempted silent coup. It all started in the summer of 2016 as Hillary Clinton was being investigated for maintaining a private email server in her home's basement that had classified information on it. This is illegal. She was asked by Congress to forward some emails to a committee, but she wiped them so they could never be recovered.[46]

On July 5, 2016, James Comey, the director of the FBI, provided a list of evidence against Mrs. Clinton, but then said she had no malintent and no reasonable prosecutor would file charges, which was highly debatable. One piece of evidence was real classified emails being found on her server.[47] An exoneration letter was actually drafted by the FBI before it interviewed Clinton. Lisa Page, who was an attorney at the FBI and was caught up in the scandal along with Peter Strzok, testified to a congressional committee behind closed doors that the Obama Justice

Department, headed by Loretta Lynch, told them (the FBI) to stand down and not charge Clinton.[48]

The text messages of Lisa Page and Peter Strzok, who were also involved in an extramarital affair, revealed that leaders in the FBI had biased feelings against Trump and wanted to help prevent him from becoming president. Besides the email server issue, then Secretary of State Clinton was involved in a very questionable uranium deal that allowed a Russian to buy 20 percent of our uranium, the substance that is used to make nuclear weapons. The Clintons established the Clinton Foundation after they left the White House following Bill Clinton's second term. The foundation collected large sums of money that were to be used for charity work around the world. It basically functioned as an expense fund for the Clintons and a means to increase personal wealth. After the Uranium One deal, the Clinton Foundation received a donation of $145 million from a Russian company connected to Uranium One.[49] Many of the donations to the Clinton Foundation appear questionable in light of Hillary serving as secretary of state and planning a run for the presidency.

The FBI turned its attention next to Donald Trump. It sought to discredit him and make him unelectable. It did so with no probable cause. There was no evidence of collusion between Russia and Trump, but that did not stop the FBI and other sources from trying to build a case for this. The all-important item for the case was a dossier created by British spy Christopher Steel. He would testify later in England that even *he* did not believe that the document was truthful. High-ranking FBI investigators, including the assistant director, were told that the dossier was not reliable, was paid for by Hillary Clinton's campaign, and was politically motivated to dig up dirt on Trump's candidacy.[50]

This unverified dossier was used fraudulently by the FBI to obtain a FISA warrant, which allowed the FBI to wiretap and view emails of a Trump foreign policy adviser, Carter Page.[51] FBI Director Comey signed off on the first FISA application and then told President-elect Trump that it was fallacious. The question is, If Comey knew it was dubious, why did he allow it to be used for getting a FISA warrant and sign off on it himself? There were three more renewals of the FISA warrant that continued into Trump's term in office. Watergate was a poorly conceived and executed break-in that happened one night. This operation launched on Trump by the FBI was called Crossfire Hurricane and was ongoing for months.

President Trump, on the recommendation of Deputy Attorney General Rod Rosenstein, fired Comey due to his handling of the Clinton case. Comey took documents of a meeting he had with President Trump and leaked them to a professor of law at New York University so that a special counsel would be appointed to investigate Russian collusion and any obstruction of justice related to it.[51]

No proof of collusion was found by Congressional committees by the special counsel after twenty-two months of investigation and 30 million dollars. And, to think that it was all based on a dossier that they all knew to be bogus. Mr. Jarrett's book, *The Russia Hoax*, is appropriately named. It is absolutely appalling that our own FBI would be used to fabricate an investigation on a presidential candidate and later a president, and help a special counsel be appointed when no grounds existed for such an appointment because no evidence of a crime existed. The fact this corruption has the fingerprints and DNA of the Democratic

Party all over it is atrocious, and there are even indications it has ties to the Obama White House.

In his First Inaugural Address, Thomas Jefferson said, "Equal and exact justice to all men, of whatever persuasion, religious or political."[52] Let's hope that his words will prove to be true, that truth comes out of this fiasco of Russian collusion and that those who have perpetrated this corruption will be held accountable. They have cost the nation millions of dollars and undeserved unrest. The special counsel investigation, which had no legal ground to be established, was basically an attempt to cover the wrongdoing by the Clinton campaign and the Obama Justice Department to illegally surveille Donald Trump the candidate and Donald Trump the president.

Space does not allow to describe in detail other corruption generated by liberals. The National Education Association (public school teachers' union) is biased toward the liberal agenda. Schools have become liberal indoctrination camps paid for by taxpayers. Colleges are dominated by liberal professors and political positions. Dr. Carol Swain and coauthor Steve wrote a book entitled *Abduction: How Liberalism Steals Our Children's Hearts and Minds.* They give a chapter each to the corruption in the public schools and in colleges.

Other topics of corruption advanced by Democrats are how the DNC fixed the 2016 presidential primary election victory for Hillary Clinton; how Hollywood slants movies and TV shows to favor liberals; ridiculous regulations on business; the attacks on the religious freedom of people running a business; the cozy relationships with unions and their shady practices; and the special favoritism extended to Planned Parenthood, which receives a half billion dollars of taxpayers' money each year. If you are a Bible-believing Christian and oppose abortion, you are required to support Planned Parenthood whether you like it or not. I believe that any organization, including schools and state colleges, that receives tax dollars should be politically neutral and be heavily fined if they violate this neutrality.

Ignoring the Fourteenth Amendment

The last focus on corruption is one that is an absolute atrocity. It is infanticide, which Democrats have gone on record in the Senate and House to support. In the winter of 2019, this issue became front-page news as the State of New York passed legislation that would allow babies who survived an abortion to not receive medical attention and be left to die.[53] This atrocity was matched by Governor Ralph Northam of Virginia during an appearance on a talk show when he spoke about a similar proposed bill in Virginia. In response to a question about a possible scenario where a baby would be born alive as the result of a botched abortion, the governor calmly said:

> If a mother is in labor, I can tell you exactly what would happen. The infant would be delivered. The infant would be kept comfortable. The infant would be resuscitated if that's what the mother and the family desired, and then a discussion would ensue between the physicians and the mother. So I think this was really blown out of proportion.[54]

Here is a governor, himself a medical doctor, going against the Hippocratic Oath he took when he became a doctor. The oath contains the following words: "I will apply all measures for the benefit of the sick according to my ability and judgment; I will keep them from harm and injustice." It does not appear the baby accidentally born will be safe from harm or injustice if Governor Northam gets his way.

This controversial issue moved on to the US Senate where a bill to protect these babies was placed on the floor for a vote. There were forty-four Democratic senators who voted against the bill.[55] This is unbelievable. Forty-four senators believe it is proper to allow a live born baby to die for the sole reason that it was supposed to be aborted. Remember the Fourteenth Amendment that reads:

> All persons born or naturalized in the United States, and subject to the jurisdiction thereof, are citizens of the United States and of the state wherein they reside. No state shall make or enforce any law which shall abridge the privileges or immunities of citizens of the United States; nor shall any state deprive any person of life, liberty, or property, without due process of law; nor deny to any person within its jurisdiction the equal protection of the laws.

It says "all persons born." It does not state any circumstances of the birthing process that creates an exemption. These babies, whom forty-four senators and other liberals want to terminate, are legal citizens of the United States. To take the life of an American citizen without due process is unconstitutional and in this case an unjustified killing. When a senator is sworn into office he or she takes an oath swearing to "support and defend the Constitution." If you are in favor of the willful termination of an innocent American citizen, you cannot be supporting or defending the Constitution. I believe that the forty-four senators who voted against this bill to protect the lives of the born babies of botched abortions have failed to live up to their oath and deserve to be removed from office. The forty-four senators are more concerned about appeasing the pro-abortion lobbyists and advocates than they are about protecting the lives of real American citizens as they are instructed to by the Constitution. This is corruption of the highest degree, when one is willing to terminate a life to please a voting group.

Conclusion

If the liberal Democrats could have their way, they would change voting laws and procedures so they would never lose another election for president and always have control of the House and Senate. They would then transform our nation into a country far from the original intent of our founders and our liberty would evaporate. Socialism has never worked. They want to embrace it. We have used the word "liberal" throughout the book and you can regard every Democrat as a liberal. They prefer the term "progressive." It sounds so much more positive. Everyone likes progress.

However, when you want to take the economy back to an elite ruling class and a large underclass of people denied opportunities of advancement and wealth creation, you are returning to an economic model closer to the feudal system. That is not progress. When the founding documents speak of the right to life and then you are willing for innocent babies to die, that is not progress. Democrats want to replace the American Dream with the liberal scheme. As they go forward duping as many uninformed voters as possible, their cohorts and comrades in the media will help them along.

What should we who love liberty and believe in a God who blessed this nation do?

1. Vote for the best party and the best candidates. Today, that party is not the Democratic Party as long as it supports the taking of the lives of unborn children and pushes such absurd policies as demanding that males be allowed to use female locker rooms, restrooms, and showers and even compete in girls' athletics. We are often told that we should vote for the best man or woman. That sounds solid but may not be so wise given the way our political system works. The party who holds the majority in the House and the Senate controls the committees, and the speaker of the House and the majority leader of the Senate decide what bills make it to the floor for a vote. You can have a candidate whom you feel represents you perfectly, but only what the chamber leader wants matters. We must vote for the best party and at this time in our republic, we don't believe it's the Democratic Party. If you don't like either party, then if people ask if you are a Republican, just tell them, "No, I just vote that way on election day." The Republican Party has been very disappointing at times, but they are currently closer to the original intent of the founders than the Democrats have become.

2. Vote your faith on issues. Many states allow voters to approve or disapprove various issues. Some of these issues can become amendments to the state constitution. They can relate to gambling issues, abortion restrictions, the legalization of certain drugs, and others that deal with cultural quality of life. You must become informed on the issues and vote in a way that best represents Christian values and biblical standards.

3. Get active. You need to become informed and involved. Learn the best sources to obtain news that does not have a liberal bias. Communicate with your representatives and government officials. The Internet makes this easy. Share with others what you have learned and if they are not registered, have them register to vote. Make sure they vote. If evangelicals would register and vote, the Democrats could not win the White House or control Congress. Make contributions to candidates you know believe in Christian values. They need not be in your district or state. And, always pray for God to move and revive our nation. If we were to have a Third Great Awakening in the country, which would have a major spiritual impact, it would change our political landscape and bring us closer to what our founders had in mind for our nation.

It's a shame that the Democratic Party has moved so far left and become more of an anti-American movement than a political party. It is far from what its founder, Thomas Jefferson, had in mind, and I have doubts JFK or Harry Truman could embrace it, given its socialist trend. Their candidates, like William Jennings Bryant and Grover Cleveland, would find today's Democrats a strange lot indeed. It would be great to see some Democratic candidates put forth the effort to reform their party and bring it back to the center and, more importantly, to the principles established by the founders, but it looks like that is wishful thinking. Right now it is just not safe to vote Democrat, if you seek to have a country friendly to the Christian message, dedicated to free markets, and supportive of the Constitution.

Honor, justice, and humility, forbid us tamely to surrender that freedom which we received from our gallant ancestors, and which our innocent posterity have a right to receive from us.[56]

—Thomas Jefferson

A wise and frugal government, which shall restrain men from injuring one another, shall leave them otherwise free to regulate their own pursuits of industry and improvement, and shall not take from the mouth of labor the bread it has earned.[57]

—Thomas Jefferson

Righteousness exalts a nation, but sin condemns any people.

—Proverbs 14:34

End Notes

Introduction

1. Mark R. Levin, *Liberty and Tyranny: A Conservative Manifesto*, Threshold Editions, New York, 2009, p 34.

2. Gouverneur Morris, letter to George Gordon, June 28, 1792.

3. John Adams, *A Defense of the Constitutions of Governments of the United States of America, 1787*

4. James Madison, Federalist No. 37, January 11, 1788.

5. David Krayden, "Eric Holder: When Did You Think America Was Great?" *Daily Caller*, March 29, 2019, https://dailycaller.com/2019/03/29/eric-holder-america-never-great-maga/

Chapter 1

1. Celeb Johnson's Mayflower.com, http://mayflowerhistory.com/voyage

2. *Religion and the Founding of the American Republic America as a Religious Refuge: The Seventeenth Century, Part 1*, https://www.loc.gov/exhibits/religion/rel01.html

3. Ibid.

4. Sue Roe, "The Quakers," http://www.genealogytoday.com/columns/recipes/tip13c.html

5. "The History of the Persecutions Suffered by the Early Quakers," http://www.hallvworthington.com/Persecutions/Persecutions1A.html

6. Ebenezer Hazard, ed., *Historical Collections; Consisting of State Papers, and Other Authentic Documents; Intended as Materials for a History of the United States of America*, vol. 1 (Philadelphia: T. Dobson, 1792), 72; David Barton, *Original Intent: The Courts, the Constitution, and Religion* (Aledo, TX: Wall Builders' Press, 2008), 76–78.

7. Hazard, *Historical Collections*, vol. 1, 252; Barton, *Original Intent*, 76–78.

8. Ebenezer Hazard, ed., *Historical Collections; Consisting of State Papers, and Other Authentic Documents; Intended as Materials for an History of the United States of America*, vol. 2 (Philadelphia: T. Dobson, 1792), 612; Barton, *Original Intent*, 76–78.

9. *The Code of 1650, Being a Compilation of the Earliest Laws and Orders of the General Court of Connecticut* (Hartford, CT: Silus Andrus, 1822), 11.

10. *The Rebirth of America* (n.p.: Arthur S. DeMoss Foundation, 1986), 41.

11. https://www.harvard.edu/about-harvard/harvard-glance/history/historical-facts

12. *America*, vol. 2:155-157; quoted at BYU: *Educational Leadership and Foundations*, "Founding of Harvard College" (http://education.byu.edu/edlf/archives/prophets/founding_fathers.html, September 26, 2012).

13. Dr. Georgia Purdom, "Harvard: No Longer 'Truth for Christ and the Church,'" *Answers in Genesis*, October 11, 2011, https://answersingenesis.org/blogs/georgia-purdom/2011/10/11/harvard-no-longer-truth-for-christ-and-the-church/

14. http://www.wm.edu/about/history/

15. *William and Mary Rules* (Richmond, VA: Augustine Davis, 1792). 6; Barton, *Original Intent*, 82.

16. "Controversial College of William and Mary President Resigns," *Fox News*, February 12, 2008. http://www.foxnews.com/story/2008/02/12/controversial-college-william-and-mary-president-resigns.html

17. Yale Charter, https://www.yale.edu/about-yale/traditions-history,

18. History of Yale, https://www.allabouthistory.org/history-of-yale.htm

19. *The Laws of Yale-College, in New Haven, in Connecticut, Enacted by the President and Fellows*, chapter 2, article 1, 4 (New Haven, CT: Josiah Meigs, 1787), 5–6; Barton, *Original Intent*, 82–83.

20. Jeffry H. Morrison, *John Witherspoon and the Founding of the American Republic* (2005)

21. https://www.princeton.edu/~oktour/virtualtour/french/Info09-Flag.htm

22. https://www.princeton.edu/meet-princeton/history#c2000s

23. https://www.columbia.edu/content/history

24. https://www.quora.com/Why-is-Columbias-motto-In-lumine-Tuo-videbimus-lumen-In-Thy-light-shall-we-see-the-light

25. *Columbia Rules* (New York: Samuel London, 1785), 5–8; Barton, *Original Intent*, 84

26. Benjamin Rush, "Thoughts upon the Mode of Education Proper in a Republic," 1806.

27. "Significance of the Great Awakening: Roots of Revolution" http://www.great-awakening.com/roots-of-revolution/

28. Robert W. Caldwell III, *Theologies of the American Revivalists*, Inter Varsity Press, Downers Grove, IL, 2017   p.17

29. Benjamin Franklin, *The Autobiography of Benjamin Franklin* (Philadelphia: J. B. Lippincott & Co, 1869), 253.

30. Daniel N. Gullotta, "The Great Awakening and the American Revolution, August 2016. https://allthingsliberty.com/2016/08/great-awakening-american-revolution/

31. Thomas S. Kidd, *The Great Awakening: A Brief History with Documents*, Bedford/St. Martin's, 2008, p. 55.

32. Frank Lambert, *Pedlar in Divinity: George Whitefield and the Transatlantic Revivals, 1737-1770* (Princeton: Princeton University, 1994), 128.

33. Daniel N. Gullotta, "The Great Awakening and the American Revolution, August 2016.   https://allthingsliberty.com/2016/08/great-awakening-american-revolution/

34. John Adams to Hezekiah Niles, February 13, 1818, *The Works of John Adams*, vol. X, ed. Charles Francis (Boston: Little, Brown, and Company, 1850-6). 282.

35. Thomas S. Kidd, *The Great Awakening: The Roots of Evangelical Christian in Colonial America*, Yale University Press. New Haven, 2007. p. 294.

36. Alice M. Baldwin, *The New England Clergy and the American Revolution* (New York: Frederick Ungar, 1958), p. 170.

37. Benjamin Franklin Morris, *Christian Life and Character of the Civil Institutions of the United States* (Philadelphia: George W. Childs, 1864), pp. 334-335.

38. *Historical and Political Reflections on the Rise and Progress of the American Rebellion* [page 54] - [page 55] Joseph Galloway, London: G. Wilkie, 1780. Rare Book and Special Collections Division, Library of Congress (81), https://www. loc.gov/exhibits/religion/rel03.html

39. Thomas Jefferson, *Declaration of Independence*, Philadelphia, July 4, 1776.

Chapter 2

1, *The Declaration of Independence*, Philadelphia, 1776

2. George Washington, *Letter to John Armstrong*, March 11, 1792

3. George Washington, *First Inaugural Address*, April 30, 1789.

4. Michael Medved, *The American Miracle: Divine Providence in the Rise of the Republic*, Crown Forum, 2016, p. 52.

5. Jacopo della Quercia, "6 Real Historic Battles Decided by Divine Intervention," December 15, 2010, http://www.cracked.com/article_18894_6-real-historic-battles-decided-by-divine-intervention.html

6. Kevin Mooney, "The Real Story of George Washington's Decisive Christmas Attack at Trenton" *The Daily Signal*, January 11, 2015, https://www.dailysignal.com/2015/01/11/patriots-celebrate-the-real-story-of-washingtons-decisive-christmas-attack-at-trenton/

7. http://www.oneidaindiannation.com/revolutionarywar/

8. Ibid.

9. Willman Sawyer, "The Oneida Nation in the American Revolution," https://www.nps.gov/fost/learn/historyculture/the-oneida-nation-in-the-american-revolution.htm

10. Janelle Pavao, "Battle of Yorktown, Virinia, " 2010-2017, https://www.revolutionary-war.net/battle-of0yorktown.html

11. Medved. p. 90.

12. "The First Congress and the First Bible," http://teachourhistory.com/first-bible.htm

13. Northwest Ordinance, Article III, Congress, July 13, 1787.

14. Benjamin Rush, *Essays*, "A Defense of the Use of the Bible as a School Book." 1806, pp. 94, 100.

15. Letter of Samuel Adams to John Adams, October 4, 1790," in *The Writings of Samuel Adams*, ed. Harry A. Cushing (New York: Octagon Books, Inc., 1968), 4:343.

16. Cited in Harry A. Warfel (Ed.), *Letters*. To David McClure, October 25, 1836. New York: NY: Library Publishers. pp. 453-454.

17. Samuel James Smith, "The New-England Primer," https://www.britannica.com/topic/The-New-England-Primer

18. Alexis de Tocqueville, *Democracy in America*, 1835-40,

19. Ibid.

20. Ibid.

21. Ibid.

22. Daniel Walker Howe, *What Hath God Wrought: the Transformation of America, 1815-1848*, Oxford University Press, New York, 2007, p. 166.

23. Ibid.

24. Howe, p. 168.

25. Howe, p. 170.

26. Ibid. and Charles Hambrick-Stowe, *Charles G. Finney and the Spirit of America Evangelism* (Grand Rapids, Mich., 1996) p. 1-21. Charles G. Finney, *Autobiography* (Westwood, N.J.,1908; orig. pub. as *Memoirs*, 1876). 21-14.

27. Howe, p. 172.

28. Ibid.

29. Howe, p. 174.

30. Howe, p.175.

31. Douglas Foster, et al., *The Encyclopedia of the Stone-Campbell Movment* (2005)

32. Whitney R. Cross, *The Burned-over District: The Social and Intellectual History of Enthusiastic Religion in Western New, 1800–1850* (1951).

33. Alice Felt Tyler, *Freedom's Ferment: Phases of American Social History from the Colonial Period to the Outbreak of the Civil War* (1944).

34. Timothy L. Smith, *Revivalism and Social Reform: American Protestantism on the Eve of the Civil War* (1957).

35. Martin Kelly, "The Second Great Awakening," March 8, 2017, https://www.thoughtco.com/the-second-great-awakening-104220

36. Carlton, Evan (2006). *Patriotic Treason: John Brown and the Soul of America*. New York, NY: Free Press.

37. "John Brown," https://www.history.com/topics/john-brown, Eric Foner and John A. Garraty, Editors. Copyright © 1991 by Houghton Mifflin Harcourt Publishing Company. All rights reserved.

36. Carlton, Evan (2006). *Patriotic Treason: John Brown and the Soul of America*. New York, NY: Free Press.

37. "John Brown," https://www.history.com/topics/john-brown, Eric Foner and John A. Garraty, Editors. Copyright © 1991 by Houghton Mifflin Harcourt Publishing Company. All rights reserved.

38. Ibid.

39. Charles G. Finney, *Memoirs* (New York: A.S. Barnes, 1876), 324.

40. "28d. Harriet Beecher Stowe — *Uncle Tom's Cabin*" US History.org, http://www.ushistory.org/us/28d.asp

41. Ibid.

42. Marjorie J. Spruill, "The Woman Suffrage Movement in the United States," *America in Class*, 1993, http://americainclass.org/wp-content/up-loads/2012/05/WEB-Woman-Suffrage-Presentation.pdf

43. http://www.specialneedsinmusic.com/folk_song_pages/battle_hymn.html

44. Ibid.

45. John Jay, *Letter to John Murry*, October 12, 1816.

46. Vidal v. Girard's Executors, 1844.

47. *Holy Trinity v. United States*, 1892.

48. Brewer, David (1905). *The United States: A Christian Nation*. The John C. Winston Company. p. 12.

49. Harry S. Truman, "Exchange of Messages with Pope Pius XII" *American Presidency Project*, August 6, 1947.

50. John Adams, *Letter to Thomas Jefferson*, June 28, 1813.

51. George Washington, *First Inaugural Address*, April 30, 1789.

52. John Dickinson, "An Address to the Committee of Correspondence in Barbados," 1766

53. Benjamin Rush, Letters of Benjamin Rush, L. H. Butterfield, editor (Princeton, New Jersey: American Philosophical Society, 1951, Vol. I, p. 475, to Elias Boudinot on July 9, 1788.

54. John Witherspoon, Address to Princeton students, May 17, 1776.

55. "God in Our Nation's Capitol," January 29, 2007. https://probe.org/god-in-our-nations-capital/

56. Newt Gingrich, *Rediscovering God in America: Reflections on the Role of Faith in Our Nation's History and Future* (Nashville, TN: Integrity House, 2006) p. 87.

57. "God in Our Nation's Capitol," January 29, 2007. https://probe.org/god-in-our-nations-capital/

58. Ibid.

59. Ibid.

60. Ibid.

61. Ibid.

62. Quotation on the Jefferson Memorial. https://www.monticello.org/site/jefferson/quotations-jefferson-memorial

63. "State Symbols USA." https://statesymbolsusa.org/symbol-or-officially-designated-item/state-motto/god-we-trust

64. Ibid.

65. Ibid.

66. "The Pledge of Allegiance and Our Flag of the United States". *Their History and Meaning*. Archived from the original on 2006-09-23. Retrieved 2014-01-08.

Chapter 3

1. Gregory A. Smith and Jessica Martínez, "How the faithful voted: A preliminary 2016 analysis," *Fact Tank*, Pew Research Center, November 9, 2016. http://www.pewresearch.org/fact-tank/2016/11/09/how-the-faithful-voted-a-preliminary-2016-analysis/

2. Ibid.

3. Ed Kilgore, "Americans With No Religion Greatly Outnumber White Evangelicals," *New York Magazine*, May 11,2018. http://nymag.com/daily/intelligencer/2018/05/the-irreligious-now-outnumber-white-evangelicals-in-america.html

4. Letter from the Danbury, Connecticut, Baptist Association to Thomas Jefferson, October 7, 1801, housed in the Thomas Jefferson Papers Manuscript Division, Library of Congress, Washington, DC.

5. Thomas Jefferson, *The Writings of Thomas Jefferson*, vol. 16 (Washington, DC: Thomas Jefferson Memorial Association of the United States, 1903), 281–282.

6. Ibid.

7. Thomas Jefferson, *The Writings of Thomas Jefferson*, vol. 19 (Washington, DC: Thomas Jefferson Memorial Association of the United States, 1903), 449–450.

8. Ibid.

9. Thomas Jefferson, *Memoirs, Correspondence, and Private Papers of Thomas Jefferson*, vol. 4 (London: Colburn and Bentley, 1829), 367.

10. Jefferson, *The Writings of Thomas Jefferson*, vol. 16, 291.

11. Joseph Story, *Commentaries on the Constitution*, vol. 3, paragraph 1871, as quoted by The Founders' Constitution, "Amendment I (Religion)," document 69, accessed February 10, 2016, http://press-pubs.uchicago.edu/founders/documents/amendI_religions69.html.

12. Thomas Jefferson, *Memoirs, Correspondence, and Private Papers of Thomas Jefferson*, vol. 3 (London: Coburn and Bentley, 1829), 441.

13. Kate Mason Rowland, *The Life of George Mason*, vol. 1 (New York: G. P. Putnam's Sons, 1892), 244.

14. House Judiciary Committee report, March 27, 1854, as quoted by Bill Bailey, "Religion and Government, Are We a Christian Nation?," The Federalist Papers Project, accessed February 10, 2016, http://www.thefederalist papers.org/history/religion-and-government-are-we-a-christian-nation.

15. *Engel v. Vitale*, 370 US 421 (1962).

16. *Abington School District v. Schempp*, 374 US 203 (1963).

17. *Reed v. Van Hoven*, 237 F. Supp. 48 (Dist. Court, WD Michigan, 1965).

18. *Lowe v. City of Eugene*, 451 P.2d 117 (1969).

19. *Warsaw v. Tehachapi* CV F-90-404 EDP (USDC, ED Ca. 1990).

20. *Wallace v. Jaffree*, 472 US at 103 (1985).

21. *Roberts v. Madigan*, 921 F. 2d 1047 (10th Circuit, 1990).

22. *Washegesic v. Bloomingdale Public Schools*, 33 F. 3d 679 (6th Circuit, 1994).

23. *Florey v. Sioux Falls School District*. 49-5, 464 F. Supp. 911 (Dist. Court, D South Dakota, 1980).

24. *Wallace v. Jaffree*, 472 US at 103 (1985), Rehnquist (dissenting).

25. Thomas Jefferson, *The Writings of Thomas Jefferson*, vol. 15 (Washington, DC: Thomas Jefferson Memorial Association of the United States, 1903), 277.

26. John Corson, "The Cultural War: The Far Left's Agenda," *Corson*, 2014. http://corson.org/archives/culture/C1_april.htm

27. The CNN Wire Staff, "California governor signs bill requiring schools to teach gay history," July15, 2011. http://www.cnn.com/2011/US/07/14/california.lgbt.education/index.html

28. David Limbaugh, *Persecution: How Liberals Are Waging War Against Christianity* (Washington, DC: Regnery, 200), 76.

29. Ibid.

30. Emma Green, "The Fear of Islam in Tennessee Public Schools," Dec 16, 2015, *The Atlantic https://www.theatlantic.com/education/archive/2015/12/fear-islam-tennessee-public-schools/420441/*

31. Carey Lodge, "California school bans all Christian Books," September 29, 2014. https://www.christiantoday.com/article/california-school-bans-all-christian-books/41072.htm

32. Ibid.

33. Ibid.

34. Ibid

35. Colin Gunn, *IndoctriNation* film, www.indoctrinationmovie.com.

36. "Banned From Showing Students the Declaration of Independence," FoxNews.com, partial transcript for *Hannity & Colmes*, November 29, 2004, accessed January 23, 2016, http://www.foxnews.com/story/2004/11/30/banned from-showing-students-declaration-independence.html.

37. Ibid.

38. Douglas Kennedy, "ACLU Sues Louisiana Over Abstinence Ed," FoxNews.com, May 16, 2002, accessed February 10, 2016, http://www.fox news.com/story/2002/05/16/aclu-sues-louisiana-over-abstinence-ed.html.

39. Paul Vitz, *Censorship: Evidence of Bias in Our Children's Textbook* (Ann Arbor, MI: Servant Books, 1986), 14.

40. Bruce, *The Death of Right and Wrong, Exposing the Left's Assault on Our Culture and Values* (Roseville, CA: Prima Forum, 2003), 162–163.

41. David Limbaugh, *Persecution*, 285-286.

42. Steve Feazel and Dr. Carol M. Swain, *Abduction: How Liberalism Steals Our Children's Hearts and Minds*, (Christian Faith Publishers, Meadville, PA) 2016. p. 154. 155.

43. Ibid.

44. Prince Frederick, "Mind Matters," *The Hindu*, June 11, 2011, accessed February 10, 2016, www.thehindu.com/todays-paper/tp-features/tp-metro plus/mind-matters/article2094593.ece.

45. "TV Land Continues to Mock Christianity with New Show 'Impastor'" 4/9/2018, *One Million Moms*. https://onemillionmoms.com/current-campaigns/tv-land-continues-to-mock-christianity-with-new-show-impastor/

46. ClassicTVHits.com, "Will and Grace," accessed January 23, 2016, http://www.classictvhits.com/show.php?id=681

47. Tyler Kingkade, "Millennial Support For Gay Marriage Hits All-Time High: Pew Research Center," *Huffington Post*, 3/21/2013. https://www.huffingtonpost.com/2013/03/21/millennial-support-gay-marriage_n_2924993.html

48. Allison Kasic, "Planned Parenthood's Racy New TV ad," *Human Events*, April 26, 2006, accessed February 10, 2016, http://humanevents.com/2006/04/26/planned-parenthoods-racy-new-tv-ad/.

49. "Planned Parenthood of the St. Louis Region and Southwest Missouri TV Commercial," Planned Parenthood of the St. Louis Region and Southwest Missouri, YouTube video uploaded March 15, 2013, accessed February 10, 2016, https://www.youtube.com/watch?v=f0A12YpJK61.

50. Stephanie Samuel, "Facebook, Google, Apple Censoring Religious Speech?" *The Christian Post*, September 16, 2011. https://www.christianpost.com/news/facebook-google-apple-censoring-religious-speech-55736/

51. Todd Starnes, "City of Houston demands pastors turn over sermons," *Fox News*, October 14, 2014. http://www.foxnews.com/opinion/2014/10/14/city-houston-demands-pastors-turn-over-sermons.html

52. "Homeschool Opposition: Who Are They? and What Do They Want?" http://www.heir.org/oldsite/oppwho.htm

53. Marc A. Thiessen, "Hillary Clinton is a threat to religious liberty." *The Washington Post*, October 13, 2016. https://www.washingtonpost.com/opinions/hillary-clinton-is-a-threat-to-religious-liberty/2016/10/13/878cdc36-9150-11e6-a6a3-d50061aa9fae_story.html?utm_term=.c30e69a0702c

54. G.W.F. Hegel, *Philosophy of Law* in Jacob Loewenberg (ed.), *Hegel: Selections* (New York: C. Scribner's Sons, 1929), pp. 443-444, 44

Chapter 4

1. John Kenneth Galbraith, *The Affluent Society and Other Writings 1952-1967*, 2010, Penguin Group (USA), p. 676

2. Galbraith, p. 677.

3. Merriam-Webster https://www.merriam-webster.com/dictionary/capitalism

4. http://www.learnersdictionary.com/definition/free%20market

5. Allan H. Meltzer, *Why Capitalism?*, Oxford University Press, New York, 2012, p.ix.

6. Martin Kelly, "Mercantilism and Its Effect on Colonial America," September 28. 2017, *ThoughtCo*, https://www.thoughtco.com/what-is-mercantilism-104590

7. Kelly, and "Alexander Hamilton's Final Version of the Report on the Subject of Manufactures, December 5, 1791," National Archives, accessed June 27, 2015.

8. John Evans, "The Pilgrims Failed Experiment with Socialism Should teach America a Lesson," Off the *Grid News*, https://www.offthegridnews.com/religion/the-pilgrims-failed-experiment-with-socialism-should-teach-america-a-lesson/

9. Ibid.

10. Ibid.

11. *Merriam-Webster*, https://www.merriam-webster.com/dictionary/socialism

12. "Benjamin Franklin Biography," The Biography.com website, https://www.biography.com/people/benjamin-franklin-9301234

13. Ibid.

14. John Locke; *Second Treaties on Civil Government*, 1690

15. Michael Sabo, "The Sacrifices Made by the Men Who Signed the Declaration," *The Daily Signal*, July 1, 2016, www.dailysignal.com/2016/07/01/the-sacrifices-made-by-the-men-who-signed-the-declaration/

16. Kristina Zucchi, May 3, 2017 "The Main Characteristics of Capitalist Economies" *Investopedia*, https://www.investopedia.com/articles/investing/102914/main-characteristics-capitalist-economies.asp

17. Alexander Hamilton, *Federalist, no. 84, 575—81*, May 28, 1788

Chapter 5

1. Donald L. Miller and Louis P. Masur, "Program 7: The Rise of Capitalism/The Invisible Hand," Annenberg Learner, *A Biography of America*, 2000. https://www.learner.org/series/biographyofamerica/prog07/transcript/index.html

2. Ibid.

3. "The Canal Era," *U. S. History*, http://www.ushistory.org/us/25a.asp , 2018.

4. Ibid.

5. Ibid.

6. Biography.com Editors "Cornelius Vanderbilt Biography, Business Leader, Philanthropist," https://www.biography.com/people/cornelius-vanderbilt-9515195, A&E Television Networks, April 28, 2017.

7. Ibid.

8. Guy Ball, "Texas Instruments Cal-Tech: World's First Prototype Electronic Calculator," 1997, *Vintage Calculators Web Museum*, http://www.vintagecalculators.com/html/ti_cal-tech1.html

9. "First Japanese Car" *Automo Story* http://www.automostory.com/first-japanese-car.htm

10. https://about.van.fedex.com/our-story/history-timeline/history/

11. Ibid.

12. Ibid.

13. Ibid.

14. https://about.van.fedex.com/our-story/company-structure/corporate-fact-sheet/

15. Lara O'Reilly, 11 Things Hardly Anyone Knows About Nike, Nov. 4, 2014, https://www.businessinsider.com/history-of-nike-facts-about-its-50th-anniversary-2014-11

16. Ibid.

17. Ibid.

18. Ibid.

19. 35 Amazing Nike Facts and Statistics (December 2018), https://expande-dramblings.com/index.php/nike-statistics/

20. O'Reilly, 11 Things Hardly Anyone Knows About Nike, Nov. 4, 2014

21. https://corporate.walmart.com/our-story/our-history

22. Ibid.

23. Ibid.

24. Ibid.

25. Richard Kestenbaum, "Is Walmart Good or Bad for America? The Question May be Outdated," May 18, 2017, https://www.forbes.com/sites/richardkesten-baum/2017/05/18/is-walmart-good-or-bad-for-america/#27a1820822ae

26. Ibid.

Chapter 6

1. https://www.ourdocuments.gov/doc.php?flash=false&doc=51

2. David R. Henderson, "An Expert Explains the Postal Monopoly," *Foundation for Economic Education*, July 9, 2018, https://fee.org/articles/an-expert-ex-plains-the-postal-monopoly/

3. https://www.archives.gov/exhibits/charters/constitution_transcript.html

4. "General information concerning patents," https://www.uspto.gov/pat-ents-getting-started/general-information-concerning-patents

5. Child Labor Provision for Nonagricultural Occupations Under the Fair Labor Standards Act" . U.S. Department of Labor, Wage and Hour Division. July 2010. Retrieved 17 April 2012.

6. Shana Lebowitz, "Here's how the 40-hour workweek became the standard in America," Oct24, 2015. https://www.businessinsider.com/history-of-the-40-hour-workweek-2015-10

7. Ibid.

8. Ibid.

9. Milton Friedman, *Capitalism and Freedom*, University of Chicago Press, Chicago, 1962, pp 14, 15.

10. Jeffery Glen, "Communism vs Socialism," *Business Dictionary*, http://www.businessdictionary.com/article/1030/communism-vs-socialism-d1412/

11. Ibid.

12, Susan Warner, "Venezuela's Death Spiral," Gatestone Institute, September 14, 2016, https://www.gatestoneinstitute.org/8924/venezuela-death-spiral

13. "God Has Not Forgotten." *Prayer Point Volume 20, Number 5*, 2019, Samaritan's Purse, Boone, NC, p.22.

14. Ibid.

15, Vivian Sequera, "Venezuelans report big weight loss in 2017 as hunger hits," February 21, 2018, Reuters, https://www.reuters.com/article/us-venezuela-food/venezuelans-report-big-weight-losses-in-2017-as-hunger-hits-idUSKCN1G52HA

16. Danielle Kurtzleben, "Rep. Alexandria Ocasio-Cortez Releases Green New Deal Outline," Feb. 7 2019, *NPR All Things Considered*, https://www.npr.org/2019/02/07/691997301/rep-alexandria-ocasio-cortez-releases-green-new-deal-outline

17. Ibid.

18. Ibid.

19. John Eidison, "The hidden agenda behind 'climate change'" Oct 2, 2018, *American Thinker*,https://www.americanthinker.com/blog/2018/10/the_hidden_agenda_behind_climate_change.html

20. Ibid.

21. Ibid.

22. Ibid.

23. Ibid.

24. *Investor's Business Daily*, march 3, 2018, "The Stunning Statistical Fraud Behind The Global Warming Scare." https://www.investors.com/politics/editorials/the-stunning-statistical-fraud-behind-the-global-warming-scare/

25. Ibid.

26. Ibid.

27. Alex Newman, "UN IPCC Scientist Blows Whistle About Climate, Sea Level," Feb. 12, 2019, *New American*, https://www.thenewamerican.com/tech/environment/item/31472-un-ipcc-scientist-blows-whistle-on-un-climate-lies

28. Ibid.

29. "5 Statistics Showing How Capitalism Solves Poverty," *Daily Wire, March 18, 2017*, https://www.dailywire.com/news/14525/5-statistics-showing-how-capitalism-solves-poverty-aaron-bandler

Chapter 7

1. James Madison, *Federalist Paper Number 45*

2. Ibid.

3. Vice President Mike Pence in a speech in Philadelphia on February 4, 2017, https://www.whitehouse.gov/briefings-statements/remarks-vice-president-mike-pence-federalist-society/

4. Max Farrand, *The Framing of the Constitution of the United States*, Yale University Press, New Haven, 1913, pp. 18-40.

5. James Madison, *The Federalist Paper No. 51*, February 8, 1788.

6. George Washington, p. 34 of a draft of a discarded and undelivered version of his first inaugural address (30 April 1789)

7. Alexander Hamilton, *The Federalist Paper No. 33*.

8. Alexander Hamilton, Statement after the Constitutional Convention (1787), https://thefederalistpapers.org/founders/hamilton/alexander-hamilton-statement-after-the-constitutional-convention-1787

9. John Adams, Address to the Military, October 11, 1798.

10. John Jay, *Federalist Paper Number 2.*

11. James Madison, *Debates in the Federal Convention,* June 26, 1787. https://teachingamericanhistory.org/resources/convention/debates/0626-2/

12. Max Farrand, p.62.

13. Max Farrand, p. 141.

14. "The Three-Fifths Compromise," Center for the Study of Federalism. http://encyclopedia.federalism.org/index.php/Three-fifths_Compromise

15. "What was the Three-Fifths Compromise?" https://constitution.laws.com/three-fifths-compromise

16. Glen Beck and Joshua Charles, *The Original Argument*, Threshold Editions, New York, NY, 2011, p. xxx.

17. George Washington, address to the Boston Selectmen, July 28, 1795

18. James Madison, *The Federalist Paper No 37*, January 11, 1788

19. John Adams, Address to the Military, October 11, 1798

20. Thomas Jefferson, letter to David Humphreys, March 18, 1789.

21. The response is attributed to Benjamin Franklin—at the close of the Constitutional Convention of 1787, when queried as he left Independence Hall on the final day of deliberation—in the notes of Dr. James McHenry, one of Maryland's delegates to the Convention. McHenry's notes were first published in *The American Historical Review,* vol. 11, 1906, and the anecdote on p. 618.

Chapter 8

1. George Anastaplo, *The Amendments to the Constitution*, The Johns Hopkins University Press, Baltimore, 1995, p.36.

2. Anastaplo, p. 46.

3. Joeph Farinaccio, "Madison, Denominations and the First Amendment," December 14, 2002, https://chalcedon.edu/resources/articles/madison-denominations-and-the-first-amendment and James Madison in the Journal of the Virginia Convention of 1776 quoted in Norman Cousins, ed., *In God We Trust: The Religious Beliefs and Ideas of the American Founding Fathers* (New York, NY: Harper & Brothers, 1958), p. 301.

4. Anastaplo, p. 53.

5. Thomas Jefferson, Proposed Virginia Constitution, 1776

6. Samuel Adams, Massachusetts` U.S. Constitution ratification convention, 1788

7. Noah Webster, An Examination of The Leading Principles of the Federal Constitution, Philadelphia, 1787

8. "Understanding the Third Amendment," https://constitution.laws.com/american-history/constitution/constitutional-amendments/third-amendment

9. Barry Friedman and Orin Kerr, "The Fourth Amendment," https://constitutioncenter.org/interactive-constitution/amendments/amendment-iv

10. "How the TSA Legally Circumvents the Fourth Amendment," *Flying with*

Fish, November 20, 2010, https://flyingwithfish.boardingarea.com/2010/11/20/how-the-tsa-legally-circumvents-the-fourth-amendment/

11. The Editors of Encyclopedia Britannica, https://www.britannica.com/topic/due-process

12. Joseph p. Williams, "The Return to the Firing Squad," *U. S. News*, March 3, 2017, https://www.usnews.com/news/the-report/articles/2017-03-03/the-firing-squad-is-making-a-comeback-in-death-penalty-cases

13. Ryan Jaslow, "Sugary drinks over 16-ounces banned in New York City, Board of Health votes," *CBS News*, September 13, 2012, https://www.cbsnews.com/news/sugary-drinks-over-16-ounces-banned-in-new-york-city-board-of-health-votes/

14. *Congressional Record*, 49 Cong., 2d Sess., vol. XVIII, Pt. II, 1887, p. 1875.

15. Raven Clabough, "Grover Cleveland's Words Ring True for Texas Farmer," *The New American*, November 24, 2010, https://www.thenewamerican.com/culture/family/item/636-grover-clevelands-words-ring-true-for-texas-farmer

16. Robert Allen Rutland, *The Birth of the Bill of Rights 1776 – 1791*, The University of North Carolina Press, Chapel Hill, 1955, p. 230.

17. The Free Dictionary (Farlex), "Eleventh Amendment," https://legal-dictionary.thefreedictionary.com/11th+Amendment

18. Reference, "What is the Purpose of the 12th Amendment," https://www.reference.com/government-politics/purpose-12th-amendment-f7ece6ef2edf89b4

19. "Fourteenth Amendment Summary," *ThoughtCo*, https://www.thoughtco.com/us-constitution-14th-amendment-summary-105382

20. Will Kenton, "Sixteenth Amendment," *Investopedia*, December 11, 2017, https://www.investopedia.com/terms/s/sixteenth-amendment.asp

Chapter 9

1. United States Department of Agriculture, "School Meals' Healthy Hungry-Free Kids Act," Oct 5, 2017, https://www.fns.usda.gov/school-meals/healthy-hunger-free-kids-act

2. Michelle Richinick, Michelle Obama wants to cut junk food, sodas from schools," Feb 25, 2014. http://www.msnbc.com/msnbc/flotus-cut-sodasschools#50538

3. National Association of Special Education Teachers, "Perkins Vocational Education Act," 2019, https://www.naset.org/index.php?id=perkinsvocational2

4. NBC News," Federal judge in Texas strikes down Affordable Care Act," Dec 14, 2018, https://www.firstcoastnews.com/article/news/politics/federal-judgein-texas-strikes-down-affordable-care-act/77-66126a1b-27c3-495a-b837-b34703e3f1a1 270 271

5. James Madison, Alexander Hamilton, and John Jay, The Federalist Papers, 2006, Barnes and Nobles Classics, New York, p. 277-278.

6. Mark Levin, *Men in Black* (Washington, DC: Regnery Publishing, 2005), pp. 27-28.

7. Robert Yates, "Essay No. 11," Anti-federalist Papers, first published in the New

York Journal, March 20, 1788, Available at www.constitution.org.

8. Levin, *Men in Black*, pp. 30-31.

9. Levin, *Men in Black*, p. 32.

10. Thomas Jefferson, Letter to A. Coray, October 31, 1823.

11. Thomas Jefferson, Letter to William Jarvis, Sept. 28, 1820

12. Thomas Jefferson, Letter to Abigail Adams, 1804.

13. *The Reports of Committees of the Senate of the United States for the Second Session of the Thirty-Second Congress, 1852-53,* (Washington: Robert Armstrong, 1853), pp. 1-4.

14. Ibid.

15. *Engel v. Vitale*, 370 US 421 (1962).

16. *Abington School District v. Schempp*, 374 US 203 (1963).

17. *Reed v. Van Hoven*, 237 F. Supp. 48 (Dist. Court, WD Michigan, 1965).

18. *Lowe v. City of Eugene*, 451 P.2d 117 (1969).

19. *Warsaw v. Tehachapi* CV F-90-404 EDP (USDC, ED Ca. 1990).

20. *Wallace v. Jaffree*, 472 US at 103 (1985).

21. *Roberts v. Madigan*, 921 F. 2d 1047 (10th Circuit, 1990).

22. *Washegesic v. Bloomingdale Public Schools*, 33 F. 3d 679 (6th Circuit, 1994).

23. *Florey v. Sioux Falls School District*. 49-5, 464 F. Supp. 911 (Dist. Court, D South Dakota, 1980).

24. Akhil Reed Amar and Les Adams, *The Bill of Rights Primer: A Citizen's Guidebook to the American Bill of Rights*, Skyhorse Publishing, New York, 2013, p. 91.

25. "The Supreme Court and the Second Amendment: Understanding the Court's Landmark Decisions," https://ammo.com/articles/second-amendment-supreme-court-cases-guide

26. "A Little Gun History," *Rense.com*, https://rense.com//general81/ligun.htm

27. "In Re Griffiths," *Oyes*, March 7, 2019, https://www.oyez.org/cases/1972/71-1336

28. Levin, *Men in Black*, p. 111.

29. Ibid.

30. Levin, *Men in Black*, p. 131.

31. Levin, *Men in Black*, p. 136.

32. Levin, *Men in Black*, p. 55.

33. Roe v. Wade, 410 U. S. 113,116 (1972).

34. Ibid.

35. Carole Batoo, "Vanderbilt-pioneered fetal surgery procedure yields positive results," Feb 9, 2011, https://news.vanderbilt.edu/2011/02/09/vanderbilt-pioneered-fetal-surgery-procedure-yields-positive-results/

36. National Right to Life Committee, "State Homicide Laws that Recognize Unborn Victims," April 2, 2018, https://www.nrlc.org/federal/unbornvictims/statehomicidelaws092302/

37. https://www.mccl.org/single-post/2018/01/16/How-Roe-v-Wade-subverted-the-Fourteenth-Amendment-to-impose-abortion-on-demand

38. Ibid.

39. Phyllis Schlafly, *The Supremacists: The Tyranny of Judges and How to Stop Them,* (Dallas: Spence Publishing), 2004, p.76.

40. Schlafly, p. 79.

41. Mark Levin, *The Liberty Amendment: Restoring the American Republic,* (New York: Threshold Editions, 2013), pp. 49-50

Chapter 10

1. *Webster's Dictionary and Thesaurus,* (New Lanark, Scotland: Geddes & Grosset) 2002, p. 542.

2. Susan Schmidt and James V. Grimaldi, "Ney Sentenced to 30 Months In Prison for Abramoff Deals," *Washington Post,* January 20, 2007 http://www.washingtonpost.com/wp-dyn/content/article/2007/01/19/AR2007011900162.html

3. Neil A. Lewis, "Abramoff Gets 4 Years in Prison for Corruption," *The New York Times,* September 4, 2008, https://www.nytimes.com/2008/09/05/washington/05abramoff.html

4. Ed Morrissey, "How Did Solyndra Get A Sweetheart Interest Rate?" *Hot Air,* September 7, 2011, https://hotair.com/archives/2011/09/07/how-did-solyndra-get-a-sweetheart-interest-rate/

5. Ibid.

6. John R. Lott, "Where did the Stimulus Money Really Go?" *Fox News,* March 23, 2012, https://www.foxnews.com/opinion/where-did-stimulus-money-really-go

7. *Newsmax,* "Barack Obama Fast and Furious Scandal: 8 Facts You Might Not Know," *Newsmax.com,* March 9, 2019.

8. Ibid.

9. Fox News, "'Not even a smidgen of corruption': Obama downplays IRS, other scandals," *Fox News,* February 3, 2014, https://www.foxnews.com/politics/not-even-a-smidgen-of-corruption-obama-downplays-irs-other-scandals

10. Peter J. Reilly, "IRS Scandal Ends As It Began With An Apology," *Forbes,* October 27, 2017, https://www.forbes.com/sites/peterjreilly/2017/10/27/irs-scandal-ends-as-it-began-with-an-apology/#67e74342fd4b

11. David Rosenberg, "Muslims to Outnumber Jews in US by 2040," Dec 1, 2018, http://www.israelnationalnews.com/News/News.aspx/240587

12. Associated Press, "Obama Bans Terms Islam` and Jihad` From U.S. Security Document," July 7, 2010, https://www.haaretz.com/1.5478578.

13. The Editors, "What We Do Know about the Benghazi Attack Demands a Reckoning," National Review, June 28, 2016, https://www.nationalreview.com/2016/06/benghazi-scandal-hillary-clinton-state-department-obama-administration-house-committee/

14. "U S Embassy Airs Ad in Pakistan to Appease; Obama Throws Free

Speech, USA under the Bus.mp4," YouTube.com, https://www.youtube.com/watch?v=6akGlF6g-Zw and Aaron Klein, "Obama Used Taxpayer Funds in Benghazi Cover-up," *World Net Daily*, May 8, 2013, https://www.wnd.com/2013/05/obama-used-taxpayer-funds-in-benghazi-cover-up/

15. Evan McMurry, "NBC's Gregory Confronts Pelosi With 'We Have to Pass the Bill to Find Out What's In It' Clip," *Mediaite*, Nov 17, 2013, https://www.mediaite.com/tv/nbcs-gregory-confronts-pelosi-with-we-have-to-pass-the-bill-to-find-out-whats-in-it-clip/

16. Katie Pavlich, "Obamacare Architect: Yeah, We Lied to The "Stupid" American People to Get It Passed," *Townhall*, November 10, 2014, https://townhall.com/tipsheet/katiepavlich/2014/11/10/obamacare-architect-yeah-we-lied-to-the-stupid-american-people-n1916605

17. Ibid.

18. Leigh Ann Caldwell, "Obamacare Repeal Bill Fails: Three GOP Senators Rebel in 49-51 Vote," *NBC News*, July 28, 2017, https://www.nbcnews.com/politics/congress/senate-gop-effort-repeal-obamacare-fails-n787311

19. Rachael Sheffield and Robert Rector, "The War on Poverty After 50 Years," *Heritage Foundation*, September 15, 1014, https://www.heritage.org/poverty-and-inequality/report/the-war-poverty-after-50-years

20. Tom Remington, "LBJ's "War on Poverty" Hurt Black Americans," January 8, 2014, http://tomremington.com/2014/01/08/lbjs-war-on-poverty-hurt-black-americans/

21. Rachael Sheffield and Robert Rector

22. Ibid.

23. Tom Remington, "LBJ's "War on Poverty" Hurt Black Americans," January 8, 2014, http://tomremington.com/2014/01/08/lbjs-war-on-poverty-hurt-black-americans/

24. Erik Eckholm **and** Matt Apuzzo, "Darren Wilson is Cleared of Rights Violation in Ferguson Shooting," *The New York Times*, March 4, 2015, https://www.nytimes.com/2015/03/05/us/darren-wilson-is-cleared-of-rights-violations-in-ferguson-shooting.html

25. Baker Boy, "Protestors in New York: 'What do we want, Dead Cops,'" *FF Today*, December 15, 2014. http://www.fftodayforums.com/forum/topic/441857-protesters-in-ny-what-do-we-want-dead-cops/

26. Benjamin Mueller and Al Baker, "2 N.Y.P.D. Officers Killed in Brooklyn Ambush; Suspect Commits Suicide," *The New York Times*, December 20, 2014, https://www.nytimes.com/2014/12/21/nyregion/two-police-officers-shot-in-their-patrol-car-in-brooklyn.html

27. Jennifer Harper, "Media bias continues: 90% of Trump coverage in last three months has been negative, study says," *The Washington Times*, December 12, 2017, https://www.washingtontimes.com/news/2017/dec/12/media-bias-continues-90-of-trump-coverage-in-last-/

28. Ibid.

29. Tim Hains, "Lara Logan Slams Media For Becoming Left-Wing "Propagandists" With "Horseshit" Low Standards," *Real Clear Politics*, February 19, 2019, https://www.realclearpolitics.com/video/2019/02/19/lara_logan_hits_media_

for_becoming_left-wing_propagandists_horseshit_low_standards.html

30. Bernard Goldberg, *Bias,* (New York: Perennial), 2003.

31. "GOOD, BAD & UGLY: How the Media Covered False Smear of Covington Kids. Narrator voice: So Far, Mostly Ugly." *Investment Watch,* January 22, 2019 https://www.investmentwatchblog.com/good-bad-ugly-how-the-media-covered-false-smear-of-covington-kids-narrator-voice-so-far-mostly-ugly/

32. Mark J. Perry, "18 spectacularly wrong predictions made around the time of first Earth Day in 1970, expect more this year," *Carpe Diem,* April 21, 2018, http://www.aei.org/publication/18-spectacularly-wrong-predictions-made-around-the-time-of-first-earth-day-in-1970-expect-more-this-year-2/

33. Edwin J. Feulner, "Some Cold Facts," *The Heritage Foundation,* June 10, 2018, https://www.heritage.org/environment/commentary/some-cold-facts

34. https://www.commentarymagazine.com/american-society/philly-voter-fraud-allegations-race-voter-id/

35. Bill Dries, "Election Commission sorts provisional ballots on way to certifying Nov. 6 election," *Daily Memphian,* Nov 26, 2018.

36. David Mark, "Democrats have won raft of late-counted House races thanks to 2002 election law," *Washington Examiner,* Nov 21, 2018, https://www.washingtonexaminer.com/democrats-have-won-raft-of-late-counted-house-races-thanks-to-2002-election-law

37. Roxy Hamilton, "Dem House Votes In Favor Of Illegal Immigrants Voting… Vote Is Seen As Promoting Voter Fraud" *Joe for America,* March 9, 2019, https://joeforamerica.com/2019/03/dem-house-votes-in-favor-of-illegal-immigrants-voting-vote-is-seen-as-promoting-voter-fraud/

38. Public Interest Legal Foundation/Virginia Voters Alliance, *Alien Invasion in Virginia: The Discovery and Coverup of Noncitizen Registration and Voting* (September 2016), available at: https://publicinterestlegal.org/files/Report_Alien-Invasion-in-Virginia.pdf

39. CBS News, "U.S. urges Mexico to tackle "increase" in heroin trafficking," October 24, 2017, https://www.cbsnews.com/news/dea-mexico-increase-heroin-fentanyl-production/

40. Evan Kohlmann, "Confirmed Terrorist-linked illegal immigrants tried to cross southern border," *The Political Insider,* January 8, 2019, https://thepoliticalinsider.com/border-apprehension-list/

41. Samantha Chang, "Former DHS agent combating child trafficking: If politicians cared about children, they'd want the wall," Feb 1, 2019, https://www.bizpacreview.com/2019/02/01/former-dhs-agent-combating-child-trafficking-if-politicians-cared-about-children-theyd-want-the-wall-719775

42. Crime Prevention Research Center, "NEW RESEARCH: The impact of illegal aliens on crime rates, data codebook and "do file," January 17, 2018, https://crimeresearch.org/2018/01/impact-illegal-aliens-crime-rates/

43. Ed Morrissey, "Obama's Student-Loan Program $22 *Billion* In The Hole For FY2015," *Hot Air,* Feb. 5, 2015, https://hotair.com/archives/2015/02/05/obamas-student-loan-program-22-billion-in-the-hole-for-fy2015/

44. *The Washington Times,* "Clinton says she has 'both a public and a private position' on Wall Street: WikiLeaks release," Oct 8, 2016, https://www.washingtontimes.com/news/2016/oct/8/hillary-clinton-says-she-has-both-public-and-priva/

45. Rush Limbaugh, Congress Has a Slush Fund to Pay Off Sexual Harassment Claims and Nobody Calls It a Crime!" *iHeart Radio,* Dec 10, 2018, https://news.iheart.com/featured/rush-limbaugh/content/2018-12-10-rush-limbaugh-blog-congress-has-a-slush-fund-to-pay-off-sexual-harassment-claims-and-nobody-calls-it-a-crime/ and see Kelsey Snell, "Time Is Running Short For Congress' Sexual Harassment Bill," *NPR,* Dec 10, 2018, https://www.npr.org/2018/12/10/675382699/lawmakers-hope-to-reach-compromise-on-overhaul-of-sexual-harassment-claims-syste

46. Gregg Jerrett, *Summary of the Russian Hoax: The Illicit Scheme to Clear Hillary Clinton and Frame Donald Trump,* Lexington, Kentucky: Book House, 2018, p. 5.

47. Jerrett, p. 7.

48. Virgina Kruta, "Lisa Page Testimony May Have Put Obama AG Loretta Lynch in the Crosshairs," *The Daily Caller,"* March 12, 2019, https://dailycaller.com/2019/03/12/lisa-page-testimony-stings-loretta-lynch/

49. Louis Nelson, "What you need to know about Clinton and the Uranium One deal," *Politico,* Nov 14, 2017, https://www.politico.com/story/2017/11/14/hillary-clinton-uranium-one-deal-russia-explainer-244895

50. Jerrett, p. 19.

51. Jerrett, pp. 29-35.

52. Thomas Jefferson, *First Inaugural Address,* March 4, 1801.

53. Steven Ertelt, "Babies Born Alive After Abortion Can be Left to Die Under New York Law Legalizing Abortions Up to Birth," *Life News,* Jan 25, 2019, https://www.lifenews.com/2019/01/25/new-york-law-legalizing-abortions-up-to-birth-revokes-medical-care-for-babies-born-alive-after-abortions/

54. Grace Segers, "Virginia Governor Ralph Northam addresses controversial abortion comments," *CBS News,* Jan 31, 201, https://www.cbsnews.com/news/virginia-governor-ralph-northam-holds-press-conference-on-controversial-abortion-comments/

55. Valarie Richardson, "Senate Democrats block GOP anti-infanticide bill spurred by Ralph Northam comments," *The Washington Times,* Feb 4, 2019, https://www.washingtontimes.com/news/2019/feb/4/anti-infanticide-bill-blocked-senate-democrats/

56. Thomas Jefferson, Declaration of the Cause and Necessities of Taking Up Arms, July 6, 1775.

57. First Inaugural Address, March 4, 1801.

ABOUT THE AUTHORS

★

Mike Huckabee was a presidential candidate in 2008 and 2016, and was governor of Arkansas from 1997 to 2007. He is host of *Huckabee* each weekend on TBN and a Fox News Contributor. He is the author of thirteen previous books, including several New York Times bestsellers. He and his wife, Janet, live in Florida and still spend time in Arkansas. They have three grown children and six

Steve Feazel is an ordained minister in an evangelical denomination where he served as pastor. He has taught as an adjunct professor of business at various universities. He produced three award-winning faith-based documentaries on social issues including the pro-life side of abortion. Besides holding a degree from seminary, he has an MBA from Arizona State University. His first published book, entitled, *Abduction: How Liberalism Steals Our Children's Hearts and Minds*, was coauthored with Dr. Carol Swain. He and his wife, Edythe, have two grown sons and five grandchildren. They reside in Ohio. Steve's website is visionword.com.